PROTECTING YOUR PERSONAL DATA: HOW LAW ENFORCEMENT WORKS WITH THE PRIVATE SECTOR TO PREVENT CYBERCRIME

FIELD HEARING

BEFORE THE

SUBCOMMITTEE ON CYBERSECURITY, INFRASTRUCTURE PROTECTION, AND SECURITY TECHNOLOGIES

OF THE

COMMITTEE ON HOMELAND SECURITY HOUSE OF REPRESENTATIVES

ONE HUNDRED THIRTEENTH CONGRESS

SECOND SESSION

APRIL 16, 2014

Serial No. 113–65

Printed for the use of the Committee on Homeland Security

Available via the World Wide Web: http://www.gpo.gov/fdsys/

U.S. GOVERNMENT PRINTING OFFICE

88–784 PDF   WASHINGTON : 2014

For sale by the Superintendent of Documents, U.S. Government Printing Office
Internet: bookstore.gpo.gov   Phone: toll free (866) 512–1800; DC area (202) 512–1800
Fax: (202) 512–2250   Mail: Stop SSOP, Washington, DC 20402–0001

COMMITTEE ON HOMELAND SECURITY

MICHAEL T. MCCAUL, Texas, *Chairman*

LAMAR SMITH, Texas
PETER T. KING, New York
MIKE ROGERS, Alabama
PAUL C. BROUN, Georgia
CANDICE S. MILLER, Michigan, *Vice Chair*
PATRICK MEEHAN, Pennsylvania
JEFF DUNCAN, South Carolina
TOM MARINO, Pennsylvania
JASON CHAFFETZ, Utah
STEVEN M. PALAZZO, Mississippi
LOU BARLETTA, Pennsylvania
RICHARD HUDSON, North Carolina
STEVE DAINES, Montana
SUSAN W. BROOKS, Indiana
SCOTT PERRY, Pennsylvania
MARK SANFORD, South Carolina
VACANCY

BENNIE G. THOMPSON, Mississippi
LORETTA SANCHEZ, California
SHEILA JACKSON LEE, Texas
YVETTE D. CLARKE, New York
BRIAN HIGGINS, New York
CEDRIC L. RICHMOND, Louisiana
WILLIAM R. KEATING, Massachusetts
RON BARBER, Arizona
DONDALD M. PAYNE, JR., New Jersey
BETO O'ROURKE, Texas
FILEMON VELA, Texas
ERIC SWALWELL, California
VACANCY
VACANCY

BRENDAN P. SHIELDS, *Staff Director*
MICHAEL GEFFROY, *Deputy Staff Director/Chief Counsel*
MICHAEL S. TWINCHEK, *Chief Clerk*
I. LANIER AVANT, *Minority Staff Director*

———

SUBCOMMITTEE ON CYBERSECURITY, INFRASTRUCTURE PROTECTION, AND SECURITY TECHNOLOGIES

PATRICK MEEHAN, Pennsylvania, *Chairman*

MIKE ROGERS, Alabama
TOM MARINO, Pennsylvania
JASON CHAFFETZ, Utah
STEVE DAINES, Montana
SCOTT PERRY, Pennsylvania, *Vice Chair*
MICHAEL T. MCCAUL, Texas *(ex officio)*

YVETTE D. CLARKE, New York
WILLIAM R. KEATING, Massachusetts
FILEMON VELA, Texas
VACANCY
BENNIE G. THOMPSON, Mississippi *(ex officio)*

ALEX MANNING, *Subcommittee Staff Director*
DENNIS TERRY, *Subcommittee Clerk*

CONTENTS

PROTECTING YOUR PERSONAL DATA: HOW LAW ENFORCEMENT WORKS WITH THE PRIVATE SECTOR TO PREVENT CYBERCRIME

Wednesday, April 16, 2014

U.S. HOUSE OF REPRESENTATIVES,
COMMITTEE ON HOMELAND SECURITY,
SUBCOMMITTEE ON CYBERSECURITY, INFRASTRUCTURE
PROTECTION, AND SECURITY TECHNOLOGIES,
Philadelphia, PA.

The subcommittee met, pursuant to call, at 10:18 a.m., at the Paul Peck Alumni Center, Drexel University, 3142 Market Street, Philadelphia, PA, Hon. Patrick Meehan [Chairman of the subcommittee] presiding.

Members present: Representatives Meehan, Fitzpatrick, and Clarke.

Mr. MEEHAN. The Committee on Homeland Security, Subcommittee on Cybersecurity, Infrastructure Protection, and Security Technologies will come to order. We are waiting for a moment, although we will begin, because by the time I am concluded with our opening statements and other things—my partner, Ms. Clarke, the Ranking Member from New York, had a little bit of trouble with the trains this morning, but she is, I know, out of the train and on her way up, so I think we will try to get the hearing started, and I will look forward to having her make her opening statement as soon as we begin.

I am—want to first express my deep appreciation to Drexel University for allowing us to use this beautiful venue for this hearing, and to also take a moment to plug the tremendous work that Drexel University is doing with the creation of their new cyber institute, which is not only using research and development to work with—the educational sector to work with the private sector and the Government sector in identifying the newest and best ways to deal with the threat of cyber—with cybersecurity, and dealing with the threats to information, but they are also going to be training the next generation of participants in the process of helping us to create better protections. I think it is a remarkable new area, and we are very grateful to have that kind of a commitment here in this region. I know it is something shared with other universities as well, but particularly what Drexel is doing is noteworthy around the country.

I also have to make note of this, guys, and it is not customary, because of the angles of the sun, it is generally law enforcement that has people locked in rooms with lights shining in their faces. Then they, you know, then they ask the tough questions. So this is kind of turnabout. We will have to see how you enjoy that aspect of it.

At this moment I am going to ask unanimous consent for Congressman Mike Fitzpatrick to participate in the hearing. Hearing no objection, so ordered. I want to express my deep appreciation to Congressman Fitzpatrick, not only for the work that he does in the broad spectrum of issues for our region, but because Congressman Fitzpatrick is growing in his importance on the Financial Services Committee. This is an area in which he has been spending time as well, and I am very grateful for his participation. When my colleague, Ms. Clarke, arrives, I will take a moment to comment on our relationship. But allow me to begin by doing an opening statement.

I want to welcome all of the witnesses, and extend my thanks for participating in today's hearing, and I appreciate the effort taken on behalf of all of those involved in this important field hearing. This is an official Congressional hearing, as opposed to a town hall meeting, or something else that we would traditionally do, so we have to abide by certain rules of the Committee on Homeland Security, and the House of Representatives. This is as if we are sitting in the House today, so photography, and cameras and other things are limited to accredited press, and we want to make sure that we respect the decorum and the rules of the committee.

I am going to give my colleague a moment to collect herself as I do my opening statement, but I would also—I did want to take a moment while Congresswoman Clarke was here to share with you—we have had the great fortune to be working together for much of the last term on this important committee. While, certainly, there are a few occasions where we have to zealously argue for our philosophical positions, the fact of the matter is it has been a remarkable working relationship. We have had the ability to collectively identify and work on a number of issues with respect to cybersecurity, including some very substantial legislation that has passed the committee unanimously, and in a bipartisan fashion, and has been a real joy to be able to work with Congresswoman Clarke in this capacity. I want to express my deep appreciation for you taking the time to come down from New York to join with us today at this field hearing. So I will recognize myself for an opening statement.

Recent cyber breaches at retailers, including Target, Nieman Marcus, and Michael's, have once again brought the public's attention to the threat of criminals accessing their personal information. Unfortunately, such data breaches are neither new nor rare. The Target attack alone comprised the information of approximately 110 million consumers, and it could be months, or even years, before we know how many of those customers will eventually be victims of fraud. In 2012, an estimated 16.6 million Americans experienced identity theft, costing consumers nearly $25 billion, so this problem is not going away. Just last week many people learned about the so-called Heartbleed vulnerability that affects the encryption software used in many e-commerce sites.

While fraud is nothing new, the techniques and scope have risen to a new level. Our increasingly interconnected world, and the advancement of on-line shopping and banking, has made our lives much more convenient, but it has also meant that a sophisticated criminal can steal your account information without ever being in the country. In fact, the biggest hotbed of hackers is in Eastern Europe, where criminals can buy, sell, and trade various pieces of software used to attack systems and steal information.

The question then becomes: What is being done about it? From the retailers responsible for protecting the information in their systems, to the banks who are liable for fraudulent charges, to law enforcement at every level, and that means local, State, and Federal, who are charged with going after the criminals, all of the stakeholders here play a role, and are working hard to counter cyber fraud and identity theft. I add that this is an issue that is well within the boundaries of our committee, and I am pleased to be able to work with Congresswoman Clarke as we engage in a series of hearings that will unfold in dealing with this important question.

Consumers must also do their part to protect themselves. Simple steps to increase cyber hygiene including creating strong passwords and changing them regularly, using anti-virus software, and keeping it updated, and most importantly, keeping an eye out for suspicious activity on your computer, and in bank accounts. So I am looking forward to hearing from all of our witnesses about the outreach they do to inform consumers to better protect themselves.

Our first panel of witnesses is directly responsible for investigating cyber crimes at the Federal and local level. In addition to its role as the lead agency investigating the recent retail breaches, we will hear from the Secret Service about the tools at their disposal, including the National Cyber Forensics Institute, which trains local law enforcement officials to investigate and prosecute cyber crimes, the Cyber Intelligence Section that collects, analyzes, and disseminates data, and the Electronic Crimes Task Force, that brings together law enforcement, academia, and the private sector to combat computer-based threats to our financial systems and critical infrastructure.

Similarly, I am pleased to have the Federal Bureau of Investigation, who will testify about their role in investigating cyber-related crimes, and about the National Cyber Investigative Joint Task Force, which was created in partnership with the Department of Defense and the intelligence community, also including law enforcement and the private sector, to coordinate and share information. That is critical as we deal with real-time transactions.

We are also going to hear from the local level, which is vitally important, and I am pleased that District Attorney Jack Whelan of Delaware County is able to be here, and he has a criminal investigation division which leads local efforts to fight cyber crime. District Attorney Whelan will share with us thoughts on how he uses his resources to deal with the investigations which have an effect on the community, and then, in addition, how we are doing at the Federal level in coordinating and helping to engage those resources at the local level.

Our second panel will discuss efforts in the private sector to prevent and respond to cyber attacks. They are the ones on the front lines, fighting the problem, and continue to suffer significant financial losses. I know we will likely hear, 85 percent of the assets that are engaged in the world of cyber are in the hands of private entities. This partnership is more critical than perhaps any other area. I am particularly interested in hearing from them about how they interact with law enforcement, and how we can help protect their customers. I look forward to hearing from all of our witnesses today, and want to thank everybody for their attendance.

Let me just conclude by saying one last thing. There are so many different aspects of cyber. You know, we deal with the threat of terrorism on a regular basis. We have State-sponsored activities, which is quite sophisticated, and often deals with the question of cyber espionage, and other kinds of things. There is the reality that the cyber world is a new dimension for warfare. In fact, there is a great deal of activity that takes place with the Department of Defense, the intelligence community, and others that operate in that domain.

But today we are focused on, how does this question come back to the local level, to the local consumer, to the person out there, to the small businessman, to the community banker? Because in the aftermath of the major issues that we have recently seen, such as Target, we realize that real lives are affected, and so our purpose today is to focus in that unique area, and I am grateful for the tremendous witnesses we have.

So I now recognize the Ranking Minority Member of the subcommittee, the gentlelady from New York, Ms. Clarke, for any statement she may have.

Ms. CLARKE. I want to thank you, Mr. Chairman, for holding this field hearing in Philadelphia today, a place I know that is close to your heart, and I might say the City of Brotherly, and I might add "Sisterly", Love, here on the campus of Drexel University. It is certainly my honor and privilege to come, and to hear from the witnesses today, and to thank you for taking us into the field, where we will have an opportunity to really reflect on how this type of cyber activity impacts on our local communities.

Modern-day criminals increasingly rely on the internet and advanced technologies to spread their criminal operations. I think everyone would agree that the internet technology has now emerged as a key factor for the majority of organized crime activity. For instance, criminals can leverage the properties of the internet to carry out traditional street crime, such as distributing illicit drugs and sex trafficking. But what we are here to talk about today is how criminals exploit the digital world to assist crimes that are often technology-driven, including identity theft, payment card fraud, and intellectual property theft.

As we will hear today, the FBI considers high-tech crimes to be the most significant crimes confronting the United States as a Nation, and we, on the subcommittee, have shown an increasing interest in guaranteeing the Federal Government has the tools and capabilities to combat modern-day crime, particularly those with cyber components, while safeguarding privacy rights.

Today's cyber criminals make their crimes more profitable by choosing specialties, and creating cyber networks of colleagues. These types of criminals can victimize individuals and organizations alike. They generally are motivated by self-interest and profit, but cyber crimes can have public health and National security consequences, especially when cyber crimes are directed towards critical infrastructure, such as our hospitals, water systems, Governmental entities, or our Nation's financial systems.

U.S. officials face the challenging task of identifying the perpetrators of malicious cyber incidents, in which victim and criminal can be far removed from one another. The person or persons behind an incident can range from lone actors to expansive criminal networks, or even nation-states. This challenge of attribution is further compounded by the anonymity afforded by the digital realm.

It can sometimes be difficult to determine the actor's motivation. Is the criminal driven by greed or glory, in the forms of recognition among fellow criminals in the cyber world, or does the criminal have broader ideological motives? Finding the answers to these questions is key to distinguishing between cyber crimes and other cyber threats, such as cyber attacks, cyber espionage, and cyber warfare. Relevant distinctions exist between these various malicious activities in the cyber domain, just as lines have been drawn between their real-world counterparts, and today's hearing will help us understand those distinctions.

In July 2011 the Obama administration released a strategy to combat transnational organized crime, addressing converging threats to National security. This strategy provides the Federal Government's first broad conceptualization of transnational organized crime, highlighting it as a National security concern. It highlights 10 primary threat categories posed by transnational organized cyber crime, penetration of state institutions, corruption, and the threats to governance, threats to the economy, threats to U.S. competitiveness in strategic markets, the nexus between criminals, terrorists, and insurgents, expansion of drug trafficking, human smuggling, trafficking in persons, weapons trafficking, intellectual property theft, and finally, cyber crime.

The President's strategy outlies, excuse me, outlines key actions to counter the range of threats posed by building international capacity, cooperation, and partnerships, and taking shared responsibility to identify what actions Federal, State, and local entities can take to protect against the threat, and impact on transnational cyber crime.

We are here today to discuss complex prosecutorial and investigative problems that face law enforcement officials and companies when dealing with cyber crime, and I look forward to your testimony. With that, Mr. Chairman, I yield back.

Mr. MEEHAN. I want to thank the Ranking Member for her opening statement, and I want to express now my deep appreciation to my colleague from Bucks County, Congressman Fitzpatrick, for joining us today, and I recognize him for any opening statement he may like to make.

Mr. FITZPATRICK. This is an issue that affects just about every sector of our lives, sector of our industry. As the Chairman did thank Drexel University, not only for hosting us, but for your interest in the issue of cyber terrorism, for what you have done so far in teaching students, and being involved in the community, and what we know you will continue to do in the future.

The committee on which I serve, which is Financial Services, held a subcommittee hearing on this exact subject just last month, and we were also joined at the subcommittee hearing by law enforcement and financial service industry representatives, and it was a really informative hearing.

The subject of this morning's hearing is an important subject that we cannot spend enough time on. Cybersecurity has privacy, financial, law enforcement, and, quite frankly, National defense implications. This is a critical issue that is not only—that is only going to grow in importance as we come to rely even more on digital and cyber infrastructure, and cyber transactions.

During the Financial Services hearing I mentioned, the feedback that I was hearing, and from small community financial institutions back home in my district in Bucks County, Pennsylvania, was how they and their customers are increasingly concerned about cybersecurity. For them, the cost is not just the money that is stolen, but they are also responsible for notifying customers and for replacing credit cards and debit cards after the incident occurs. That takes manpower. That has material costs. These costs are borne by financial institutions of all sizes, but are disproportionately burdensome to community banks and small financial institutions, and credit unions as well.

Protecting personal information and financial data is a shared responsibility. It is going to take collaboration and cooperation among retailers, private institutions, and financial service providers. As this hearing will explore, the Government has an important role to play not only in law enforcement, but ensuring that individuals, businesses, and public property are protected. After all these are homeland security issues. It is not just criminals who are seeking to exploit security lapses, but also nation-states, and non-state enemies of the United States who could, and have, attacked our banking sectors, as well as other critical infrastructure areas.

So, again, I am very interested in this topic. I appreciate the Chairman calling the hearing here in the City of Brotherly Love, the city of Philadelphia. We are all looking forward to the testimony of the two panels today, and I appreciate the chance to participate.

Mr. MEEHAN. I thank the Congressman for being here. We are pleased as well to have two distinguished panels of witnesses before us today on this important topic. I am going to introduce the first panel, and then recognize each of you for your testimony.

First, to my left, is Mr. Ari Baranoff. He is an assistant special agent in charge of the criminal investigative division with the United States Secret Service. Mr. Baranoff has had over 19 years of Federal law enforcement experience, the majority of which has been with the Secret Service. He is currently assigned to the Secret Service headquarters in Washington, DC, and is the manager of the cyber investigations branch, where he has overseen the investigation and capture of the Secret Service's most wanted financial criminals.

Prior to assuming command of the cyber investigations branch, Mr. Baranoff led the New York Electronic Crimes Task Force, and it is a—I am greatly appreciative that you would travel from Washington to be with us here today. All of our witnesses are among the Nation's top experts in these areas.

Richard Quinn, from the Federal Bureau of Investigation, is an assistant special agent in charge here in the Philadelphia field office. He focuses on National security issues. Prior to his work in the Philadelphia field office, Mr. Quinn was an FBI counterterrorism agent in New York. Mr. Quinn witnessed the horrific attacks on the World Trade Center on September 11, 2011, and was one of five agents assigned to the primary team to investigate the aftermath. That is the kind of an incident that always lingers in our minds, and I think one day after the first anniversary of the Boston bombings as well, we still live with a very real recognition that—a lot of why we are here today, and the great work you are doing protecting our homeland from the threat of terror, in addition to things like the cyber threat.

Here from the local law enforcement community, representing his colleagues from across the region, is district attorney for Delaware County, Pennsylvania, Jack Whelan. Jack was elected in November 2011. As a district attorney, DA Whelan's responsible for the prosecution of criminal offenses within the jurisdiction of Delaware County, including homicides and drug enforcement, as well as cyber crime. Before becoming district attorney, Mr. Whelan served as the chairman of the Delaware County Council, where he took a lead on many public safety issues that focused on homeland security. I might add, the Internet Crimes Against Children Task Force is housed in the District Attorney's Office for the State-wide region in Delaware County, and it has been a mechanism by which that office, working with a consortium, has been at the cutting edge of cyber investigations across the board.

So I want to thank all of you for being here. The full written statements of the witnesses will appear in the record. So we don't have the usual demands that we might customarily have because of the size of our committee here this morning, but I will still ask you to do your best to stay within the time frames, to the extent that you can. So, at this point, I will recognize Mr. Baranoff for your opening statement.

STATEMENT OF ARI BARANOFF, ASSISTANT SPECIAL AGENT IN CHARGE, CRIMINAL INVESTIGATIVE DIVISION, UNITED STATES SECRET SERVICE

Mr. BARANOFF. Thank you, sir. Good morning, Chairman Meehan, Ranking Member Clarke, and distinguished Members of the subcommittee. Thank you for the opportunity to testify here at Drexel University on behalf of the Department of Homeland Security regarding the cyber crime threats our Nation faces, and how law enforcement works with the private sector to prevent cyber crime.

Our modern financial system depends on information technology for convenience and efficiency. Accordingly, criminals motivated by greed have adapted their methods, and are increasingly using cyber space to exploit our Nation's financial payment systems to engage in fraud and other illicit activities. The widely-reported payment card data breaches of Target, Nieman Marcus, White Lodging, and other retailers are just recent examples of this trend. The U.S. Secret Service is investigating these recent data breaches, and we are confident that we will bring the criminals responsible to justice.

However, what you don't hear in the news coverage is the numerous data breaches the Secret Service prevents by discreetly working with businesses to disrupt and thwart the plans of cyber criminals. This year is the 30th anniversary of when Congress first defined as specific Federal crimes both unauthorized access to computers and access device fraud, while explicitly assigning the Secret Service authority to investigate these crimes. Over the past 3 decades the Secret Service has continuously innovated in how we investigate these crimes to defeat the criminal organizations responsible for major data breaches.

In support of the Department of Homeland Security's mission to safeguard and secure cyber space, the Secret Service uses a variety of investigative methods to develop information regarding the most capable cyber threat actors. To prevent losses, we share information with victim companies of on-going or planned network intrusions to prevent any financial losses.

To accomplish this mission, the Secret Service currently operates a network of 35 electronic crimes task forces, which in 2001 Congress assigned the mission of preventing, detecting, and investigating various forms of electronic crimes, including potential terrorist attacks against critical infrastructure and financial payment systems. In addition, through our department's National Cybersecurity and Communications Integration Center, the NCCIC, the Secret Service also widely shares technical cybersecurity information, while protecting civil rights and civil liberties in order to enable other organizations to reduce their cyber risks by mitigating technical vulnerabilities. As a result of our cyber crime investigations over the past 4 years, the Secret Service has arrested nearly 5,000 cyber criminals. In total, these criminals were responsible for over a billion dollars in fraud losses. We estimate our investigations prevented over $11 billion in fraud losses.

Secret Service is committed to building the cybersecurity capacity of our Nation, and developing a greater understanding of cybersecurity threats. Universities and research institutions like Drexel, and its recently-opened cybersecurity institute, are critical partners of the Secret Service in these efforts. Drexel University continues to be a valued member of our Philadelphia Electronic Crimes Task Force, and this highly-productive partnership is an excellent example of the sort of relationships the Secret Service has developed with over 200 academic institutions Nation-wide to our electronic crimes task forces. The Secret Service also partners with the private sector and academia to research cyber threats, and publish information on cyber crime trends, through reports like the Carnegie-Mellon CERT Insider Threat Study, the Verizon Data Breach Investigations Report, and the Trustwave Global Security Report.

Secret Service develops the capability of State and local law enforcement to investigate cyber crime. At our National Computer Forensics Institute in Hoover, Alabama, the Secret Service trains hundreds of State and local law enforcement in methods for investigating cyber crime. Since opening in 2008, the institute has held over 150 cyber and digital forensics courses in 16 separate subjects, and trained and equipped more than 3,000 police investigators, prosecutors, and judges from all 50 States, and three U.S. territories. These graduates represent more than 1,000 agencies Nationwide, and include 52 law enforcement officials right here in the Philadelphia Metropolitan area.

Secret Service has a long history of protecting our Nation's financial system from threats. In 1865 the threat we were founded to address was that of counterfeit currency. As our financial payment system has evolved from paper, to plastic, to now digital information, so too has our investigative mission. The Secret Service is committed to continuing to protect our Nation, even as criminals increasingly use cyber space to engage in criminal activity.

Thank you for the opportunity to testify on this important topic, and I look forward to your questions.

[The prepared statement of Mr. Baranoff follows:]

PREPARED STATEMENT OF ARI BARANOFF

APRIL 16, 2014

Good morning Chairman Meehan, Ranking Member Clarke, and distinguished Members of the subcommittee. Thank you for the opportunity to testify here at Drexel University on the risks and challenges the Nation faces from cyber crime and the importance of partnering with the private sector to address these challenges. Based on the United States Secret Service's (Secret Service) 3 decades of experience investigating cyber crime and the understanding we have developed regarding the modern transnational organized cyber crime threat to our Nation, I hope to provide this subcommittee useful insight into these issue from a Federal law enforcement perspective.

THE ROLE OF THE SECRET SERVICE

The Secret Service was founded in 1865 to protect the U.S. financial system from the counterfeiting of our National currency. As the Nation's financial system evolved from paper to plastic to electronic transactions, so too has the Secret Service's investigative mission. Today, our modern financial system depends heavily on information technology for convenience and efficiency. Accordingly, criminals have adapted their methods and are increasingly using cyber space to exploit our Nation's financial payment system by engaging in fraud and other illicit activities. This is not a new trend; criminals have been committing cyber financial crimes since at least 1970.[1]

Congress promulgated 18 USC §§ 1029–1030 as part of enacting the Comprehensive Crime Control Act of 1984. Those subsections explicitly assigned the Secret Service authority to investigate these criminal violations.[2] They first established as specific Federal crimes unauthorized access to computers[3] and the fraudulent use, or trafficking of, access devices[4]—defined as any piece of information or tangible item that is a means of account access that can be used to obtain money, goods, services, or other thing of value.[5]

Secret Service investigations have resulted in the arrest and successful prosecution of cyber criminals involved in the largest known data breaches, including those of TJ Maxx, Dave & Buster's, Heartland Payment Systems, and others. Over the

---

[1] Beginning in 1970, and over the course of 3 years, the chief teller at the Park Avenue branch of New York's Union Dime Savings Bank manipulated the account information on the bank's computer system to embezzle over $1.5 million from hundreds of customer accounts. This early example of cyber crime not only illustrates the long history of cyber crime, but the difficulty companies have in identifying and stopping cyber criminals in a timely manner—a trend that continues today.

[2] See 18 USC §§ 1029(d) & 1030(d)(1).

[3] See 18 USC § 1030.

[4] See 18 USC § 1029.

[5] See 18 USC § 1029(e)(1).

past 4 years Secret Service cyber crime investigations have resulted in over 4,900 arrests, associated with approximately $1.37 billion in fraud losses and the prevention of over $11.24 billion in potential fraud losses, with a 99.5% conviction rate in cases that go to trial. Through our work with our partners at the Department of Justice (DOJ), in particular the local U.S. Attorney Offices, the Computer Crime and Intellectual Property Section (CCIPS), the International Organized Crime Intelligence and Operations Center (IOC–2), and others, we are confident we will continue to bring the cyber criminals that perpetrate major data breaches to justice.

THE TRANSNATIONAL CYBER CRIME THREAT

Advances in computer technology and greater access to personally identifiable information (PII) via the internet have created on-line marketplaces for transnational cyber criminals to share stolen information and criminal methodologies. As a result, the Secret Service has observed a marked increase in the quality, quantity, and complexity of cyber crimes targeting private industry and critical infrastructure. These crimes include network intrusions, hacking attacks, malicious software, and account takeovers leading to significant data breaches affecting every sector of the world economy. The recently reported data breaches of Target and Neiman Marcus are just the most recent, well-publicized examples of this decade-long trend of major data breaches perpetrated by cyber criminals who are intent on targeting our Nation's retailers and financial payment systems.

The increasing level of collaboration among cyber criminals allows them to compartmentalize their operations, greatly increasing the sophistication of their criminal endeavors as they develop expert specialization. These specialties raise both the complexity of investigating these cases, as well as the level of potential harm to companies and individuals. For example, illicit underground cyber crime marketplaces allow criminals to buy, sell, and trade malicious software, access to sensitive networks, spamming services, payment card data, PII, bank account information, brokerage account information, hacking services, and counterfeit identity documents. These illicit digital marketplaces vary in size, with some of the more popular sites boasting membership of approximately 80,000 users. These digital marketplaces often use various digital currencies, and cyber criminals have made extensive use of digital currencies to pay for criminal goods and services or launder illicit proceeds.

The Secret Service has successfully investigated many underground cyber criminal marketplaces. In one such infiltration, the Secret Service initiated and conducted a 3-year investigation that led to the indictment of 11 perpetrators allegedly involved in hacking nine major U.S. retailers and the theft and sale of more than 40 million credit and debit card numbers. The investigation revealed that defendants from the United States, Estonia, China, and Belarus successfully obtained credit and debit card numbers by hacking into the wireless computer networks of major retailers—including TJ Maxx, BJ's Wholesale Club, Office Max, Boston Market, Barnes & Noble, Sports Authority, and Dave & Buster's. Once inside the networks, these cyber criminals installed "sniffer" programs [6] that would capture card numbers, as well as password and account information, as they moved through the retailers' credit and debit processing networks. After the data was collected, the conspirators concealed the information in encrypted computer servers that they controlled in the United States and Eastern Europe. The credit and debit card numbers were then sold through on-line transactions to other criminals in the United States and Eastern Europe. The stolen numbers were "cashed out" by encoding card numbers on the magnetic strips of blank cards. The defendants then used these fraudulent cards to withdraw tens of thousands of dollars at a time from ATMs. The defendants were able to conceal and launder their illegal proceeds by using anonymous internet-based digital currencies within the United States and abroad, and by channeling funds through bank accounts in Eastern Europe.[7]

In data breaches like these the effects of the criminal acts extended well beyond the companies compromised, potentially affecting millions of individual card holders. Proactive and swift law enforcement action protects consumers by preventing and limiting the fraudulent use of payment card data, identity theft, or both. Cyber crime directly impacts the U.S. economy by requiring additional investment in implementing enhanced security measures, inflicting reputational damage on U.S.

---

[6] Sniffers are programs that detect particular information transiting computer networks, and can be used by criminals to acquire sensitive information from computer systems.

[7] Additional information on the criminal use of digital currencies can be referenced in testimony provided by U.S. Secret Service Special Agent in Charge Edward Lowery before the Senate Homeland Security and Governmental Affairs Committee in a hearing titled, "Beyond Silk Road: Potential Risks, Threats, and Promises of Virtual Currencies" (November 18, 2013).

firms, and direct financial losses from fraud—all costs that are ultimately passed on to consumers.

SECRET SERVICE STRATEGY FOR COMBATING THIS THREAT

The Secret Service proactively investigates cyber crime using a variety of investigative means to infiltrate these transnational cyber criminal groups. As a result of these proactive investigations, the Secret Service is often the first to learn of planned or on-going data breaches and is quick to notify financial institutions and the victim companies with actionable information to mitigate the damage from the data breach and terminate the criminal's unauthorized access to their networks. One of the most poorly understood facts regarding data breaches is that it is rarely the victim company that first discovers the criminal's unauthorized access to their network; rather it is law enforcement, financial institutions, or other third parties that identify and notify the likely victim company of the data breach by identifying the common point of origin of the sensitive data being trafficked in cyber crime marketplaces.

A trusted relationship with the victim is essential for confirming the crime, remediating the situation, beginning a criminal investigation, and collecting evidence. The Secret Service's global network of field offices, including our 35 Electronic Crimes Task Forces (ECTFs), are essential for building and maintaining these trusted relationships, along with the Secret Service's commitment to protecting victims' privacy and the confidentiality of their information.

When the Secret Service identifies a potential network intrusion, the Secret Service contacts the owner of the suspected compromised computer systems in order to assess the data breach and to stop the continued theft of sensitive information and the exploitation of a network. Once the victim of a data breach confirms that unauthorized access to their networks has occurred, the Secret Service works with the local U.S. Attorney's office, or appropriate State and local officials, to begin a criminal investigation of the potential violation of 18 USC § 1030. During the course of this criminal investigation, the Secret Service identifies the malware and means of access used to acquire data from the victim's computer network. In order to enable other companies to mitigate their cyber risk based on current cyber crime methods, we quickly share information concerning the cybersecurity incident with the widest audience possible, while protecting grand jury information, the integrity of on-going criminal investigations, and the victims' privacy and confidentiality. We share this cybersecurity information through:

- Our Department's National Cybersecurity & Communications Integration Center (NCCIC);
- The Information Sharing and Analysis Centers (ISAC);
- Our ECTFs;
- The publication of joint industry notices;
- Our numerous partnerships developed over the past 3 decades in investigating cyber crimes; and,
- Contributions to leading industry and academic reports like the Verizon Data Breach Investigations Report, the Trustwave Global Security Report, and the Carnegie Mellon CERT Insider Threat Study.

As we share cybersecurity information discovered in the course of our criminal investigation, we also continue our investigation in order to apprehend and bring to justice those involved. Due to the inherent challenges in investigating transnational crime, particularly the lack of cooperation of some countries with law enforcement investigations, occasionally it takes years to finally apprehend the top tier criminals responsible. For example, Dmitriy Smilianets and Vladimir Drinkman were arrested in June 2012, as part of a multi-year investigation by the Secret Service, while they were traveling in the Netherlands thanks to the assistance of Dutch law enforcement. The alleged total fraud loss from their cyber crimes exceeds $105 million.

As a part of our cyber crime investigations, the Secret Service also targets individuals who operate illicit infrastructure that supports the transnational organized cyber criminal. For example, in May 2013 the Secret Service, as part of a joint investigation through the Global Illicit Financial Team, shut down the digital currency provider Liberty Reserve. Liberty Reserve is alleged to have had more than 1 million users worldwide and to have laundered more than $6 billion in criminal proceeds. This case is believed to be the largest money laundering case ever prosecuted in the United States and is being jointly prosecuted by the U.S. Attorney's Office for the Southern District of New York and DOJ's Asset Forfeiture and Money Laundering Section. In a coordinated action with the Department of the Treasury, Liberty Reserve was identified as a financial institution of primary money laundering concern under Section 311 of the USA PATRIOT Act, effectively cutting it off from the U.S. financial system.

COLLABORATION WITH OTHER FEDERAL AGENCIES AND INTERNATIONAL LAW ENFORCEMENT

While cyber criminals operate in a world without borders, the law enforcement community does not. The increasingly multi-national, multi-jurisdictional nature of cyber crime cases has increased the time and resources needed for successful investigation and adjudication. The partnerships developed through our ECTFs, the support provided by our Criminal Investigative Division, the liaison established by our overseas offices, and the training provided to our special agents via Electronic Crimes Special Agent Program are all instrumental to the Secret Service's successful network intrusion investigations.

One example of the Secret Service's success in these investigations is the case involving Heartland Payment Systems. As described in the August 2009 indictment, a transnational organized criminal group allegedly used various network intrusion techniques to breach security and navigate the credit card processing environment. Once inside the networks, they installed "sniffer" programs to capture card numbers, as well as password and account information. The Secret Service investigation, the largest and most complex data breach investigation ever prosecuted in the United States, revealed that data from more than 130 million credit card accounts were at risk of being compromised and exfiltrated to a command-and-control server operated by an international group directly related to other on-going Secret Service investigations. During the course of the investigation, the Secret Service uncovered that this international group committed other intrusions into multiple corporate networks to steal credit and debit card data. The Secret Service relied on various investigative methods, including subpoenas, search warrants, and Mutual Legal Assistance Treaty (MLAT) requests to identify three main suspects. As a result of the investigation, these primary suspects were indicted for various computer-related crimes. The lead defendant in the indictment pled guilty and was sentenced to 20 years in Federal prison. This investigation is on-going with over 100 additional victim companies identified.

Recognizing these complexities, several Federal agencies are collaborating to investigate cases and identify proactive strategies. Greater collaboration within the Federal, State, and local law enforcement community enhances information sharing, promotes efficiency in investigations, and facilitates efforts to de-conflict in cases of concurrent jurisdiction. For example, the Secret Service has collaborated extensively with DOJ's CCIPS, which "prevents, investigates, and prosecutes computer crimes by working with other government agencies, the private sector, academic institutions, and foreign counterparts."[8] The Secret Service's ECTFs are a natural complement to CCIPS, resulting in an excellent partnership over the years. In the last decade, nearly every major cyber investigation conducted by the Secret Service has benefited from CCIPS contributions.

The Secret Service also partners with numerous international law enforcement agencies, including the FBI. For example, in August 2010, a joint operation yielded the seizure of 143 computer systems—one of the largest international seizures of digital media obtained by U.S. law enforcement—consisting of 85 terabytes of data, which was transferred to law enforcement authorities in the United States. The data was seized from a criminal internet service provider located in Odessa, Ukraine, also referred to as a "Bullet Proof Hoster."

The case of Vladislav Horohorin is another example of successful cooperation between the Secret Service and its law enforcement partners around the world. Mr. Horohorin, one of the world's most notorious traffickers of stolen financial information, was arrested while traveling in France on August 25, 2010, pursuant to a request for his provisional arrest with a view toward extradition to the United States. Mr. Horohorin created the first fully-automated on-line store which held stolen credit card data for sale. Both CCIPS and the Office of International Affairs at DOJ played critical roles in this apprehension.

Apprehending transnational cyber criminals like these is made possible by the Secret Service's 24 international field offices developing close partnerships with numerous foreign law enforcement agencies in order to combat transnational crime. To strengthen our ability to investigate transnational cyber crime, the Secret Service maintains ECTFs in London and Rome, has assigned agents to INTERPOL and EUROPOL, and operates cyber crime working groups in the Netherlands, Estonia,

---

[8] U.S. Department of Justice. (n.d.). *Computer Crime & Intellectual Property Section: About CCIPS.* Retrieved from *http://www.justice.gov/criminal/cybercrime/*.

Lithuania, Latvia, Ukraine, and Germany. The Secret Service also trains numerous international partners on investigating cyber crime; in the past 3 years the Secret Service has trained over 500 law enforcement officials representing over 90 countries in investigating cyber crimes.

The Secret Service investigations of transnational crime are facilitated by the dedicated efforts of both the Department of State and the DOJ's Office of International Affairs to execute MLATs and other forms of international law enforcement cooperation, in addition to the personal relationships that develop between Secret Service agents and their foreign counterparts through these working groups and training efforts.

Within DHS, the Secret Service benefits from a close relationship with Immigration and Customs Enforcement's Homeland Security Investigations (ICE–HSI). Since 1997, the Secret Service, ICE–HSI, and IRS–CI have jointly trained on computer investigations through the Electronic Crimes Special Agent Program (ECSAP). ICE–HSI is also a member of Secret Service ECTFs, and ICE–HSI and the Secret Service have partnered on numerous cyber crime investigations including the recent take-down of the digital currency Liberty Reserve.

To further its cybersecurity information-sharing efforts, the Secret Service has strengthened its relationship with the National Protection and Programs Directorate (NPPD), including the NCCIC. As the Secret Service identifies malware, suspicious IPs, and other information through its criminal investigations, it shares information with our Department's NCCIC. The Secret Service continues to build upon its full-time presence at NCCIC to coordinate its cyber programs with other Federal agencies.

As a part of these efforts, and to ensure that information is shared in a timely and effective manner, the Secret Service has personnel assigned to the following DHS and non-DHS entities:

- NPPD's National Cybersecurity & Communications Integration Center (NCCIC);
- NPPD's Office of Infrastructure Protection;
- DHS's Science and Technology Directorate (S&T);
- The National Cyber Investigative Joint Task Force (NCIJTF);
- Each FBI Joint Terrorism Task Force (JTTF), including the National JTTF;
- Department of the Treasury—Office of Terrorist Financing and Financial Crimes (TFFC);
- Department of the Treasury—Financial Crimes Enforcement Network (FinCEN);
- Central Intelligence Agency;
- DOJ's International Organized Crime and Intelligence Operations Center (IOC–2);
- Drug Enforcement Administration's Special Operations Division;
- EUROPOL; and
- INTERPOL.

The Secret Service is committed to ensuring that all its information-sharing activities comply with applicable laws, regulations, and policies, including those that pertain to privacy, confidentiality, and civil liberties.

SECRET SERVICE FRAMEWORK

To protect our financial infrastructure, industry, and the American public, the Secret Service has adopted a multi-faceted approach to aggressively combat cyber and computer-related crimes.

Electronic Crimes Task Forces

In 1995, the Secret Service New York Field Office established the New York Electronic Crimes Task Force (ECTF) to combine the resources of academia, the private sector, and local, State, and Federal law enforcement agencies to combat computer-based threats to our financial payment systems and critical infrastructures. In 2001, Congress directed the Secret Service to establish a Nation-wide network of ECTFs to "prevent, detect, and investigate various forms of electronic crimes, including potential terrorist attacks against critical infrastructure and financial payment systems."[9]

Secret Service field offices currently operate 35 ECTFs, including two based overseas in Rome, Italy, and London, England. Membership in our ECTFs includes: Over 4,000 private-sector partners; over 2,500 international, Federal, State, and local law enforcement partners; and over 350 academic partners. By joining our

---

[9] See Public Law 107–56 Section 105 (appears as note following 18 U.S.C. § 3056).

ECTFs, our partners benefit from the resources, information, expertise, and advanced research provided by our international network of members while focusing on issues with significant regional impact.

Cyber Intelligence Section

Another example of our partnership approach with private industry is our Cyber Intelligence Section (CIS) which analyzes evidence collected as a part of Secret Service investigations and disseminates information in support of Secret Service investigations world-wide and generates new investigative leads based upon its findings. CIS leverages technology and information obtained through private-sector partnerships to monitor developing technologies and trends in the financial payments industry for information that may be used to enhance the Secret Service's capabilities to prevent and mitigate attacks against the financial and critical infrastructures. CIS also has an operational unit that investigates international cyber criminals involved in cyber intrusions, identity theft, credit card fraud, bank fraud, and other computer-related crimes. The information and coordination provided by CIS is a crucial element to successfully investigating, prosecuting, and dismantling international criminal organizations.

Electronic Crimes Special Agent Program

A central component of the Secret Service's cyber crime investigations is its Electronic Crimes Special Agent Program (ECSAP), which is comprised of nearly 1,400 Secret Service special agents who have received at least one of three levels of computer crimes-related training.

Level I—Basic Investigation of Computers and Electronic Crimes (BICEP).—The BICEP training program focuses on the investigation of electronic crimes and provides a brief overview of several aspects involved with electronic crimes investigations. This program provides Secret Service agents and our State and local law enforcement partners with a basic understanding of computers and electronic crime investigations and is now part of our core curriculum for newly-hired special agents.

Level II—Network Intrusion Responder (ECSAP–NI).—ECSAP–NI training provides special agents with specialized training and equipment that allows them to respond to and investigate network intrusions. These may include intrusions into financial sector computer systems, corporate storage servers, or various other targeted platforms. The Level II trained agent will be able to identify critical artifacts that will allow for effective investigation of identity theft, malicious hacking, unauthorized access, and various other related electronic crimes.

Level III—Computer Forensics (ECSAP–CF).—ECSAP–CF training provides special agents with specialized training and equipment that allows them to investigate and forensically obtain digital evidence to be utilized in the prosecution of various electronic crimes cases, as well as criminally-focused protective intelligence cases.

These agents are deployed in Secret Service field offices throughout the world and have received extensive training in forensic identification, as well as the preservation and retrieval of electronically-stored evidence. ECSAP-trained agents are computer investigative specialists, qualified to conduct examinations on all types of electronic evidence. These special agents are equipped to investigate the continually evolving arena of electronic crimes and have proven invaluable in the successful prosecution of criminal groups involved in computer fraud, bank fraud, identity theft, access device fraud, and various other electronic crimes targeting our financial institutions and private sector.

National Computer Forensics Institute

The National Computer Forensics Institute (NCFI), located in Hoover, AL, is the result of a partnership between the Secret Service, NPPD, the State of Alabama, and the Alabama District Attorney's Association. The goal of this facility is to provide a National standard of training for a variety of electronic crimes investigations. The program offers State and local law enforcement officers and prosecutors the training necessary to perform computer forensics examinations, respond to network intrusion incidents, and to conduct electronic crimes investigations, while judges receive general education in these areas. Since opening in 2008, the institute has held over 150 cyber and digital forensics courses in 16 separate subjects and trained and equipped more than 3,000 State and local officials, including more than 2,300 police investigators, 840 prosecutors, and 230 judges from all 50 States and three U.S. territories. These NCFI graduates represent more than 1,000 agencies Nation-wide.

State and local agencies greatly benefit from this Secret Service-provided education on investigating cyber crime. In some of the advanced forensics and network intrusion courses, students are issued all of the hardware, software, and licenses necessary to conduct investigations. NCFI students receive the same equipment and advanced software as U.S. Secret Service special agents—a considerable benefit as it allows both the local officer and the Federal agent to operate on common systems.

Graduates of the NCFI return to their respective agencies and apply their newly-acquired skills and equipment to investigating computer-based crimes. Additionally, these graduates are offered the chance to participate in the Secret Service's Electronic Crimes Task Force (ECTF) program. State and local ECTF members work alongside other Federal agencies and private-sector entities to combat the systemic flood of cyber-related crimes targeting both private citizens and our Nation's financial infrastructure. These ECTF members also serve as force multiplier for the U.S. Secret Service ECSAP program.

Partnerships with Academia

The Secret Service has a long history of closely partnering with academia as a part of our mission. For example, Drexel University is a valued member of our Philadelphia ECTF, and this highly productive partnership to address the challenges of cyber crime is an excellent example of the sort of partnerships the Secret Service has developed with over 200 academic institutions Nation-wide through our ECTFs. The Secret Service is continually expanding its partnerships with academia through its 35 Electronic Crimes Task Forces. In addition to the numerous universities that are ECTF members, the Secret Service has a close, collaborative relationship with both Carnegie Mellon and the University of Tulsa.

In August 2000, the Secret Service and Carnegie Mellon University Software Engineering Institute (SEI) established the Secret Service CERT [10] Liaison Program to provide technical support, opportunities for research and development, as well as public outreach and education to more than 150 scientists and researchers in the fields of computer and network security, malware analysis, forensic development, training, and education. Supplementing this effort is research into emerging technologies being used by cyber-criminals and development of technologies and techniques to combat them.

The primary goals of the program are: To broaden the Secret Service's knowledge of software engineering and networked systems security; to expand and strengthen partnerships and relationships with the technical and academic communities; partner with CERT–SEI and Carnegie Mellon University to support research and development to improve the security of cyberspace and improve the ability of law enforcement to investigate crimes in a digital age; and to present the results of this partnership at the quarterly meetings of our ECTFs.

In August 2004, the Secret Service partnered with CERT–SEI to publish the first "Insider Threat Study" examining the illicit cyber activity and insider fraud in the banking and finance sector. Due to the overwhelming response to this initial study, the Secret Service and CERT–SEI, in partnership with DHS Science & Technology (S&T), updated the study and released the most recent version just last year, which is published at *http://www.cert.org/insider_threat/*.

To improve law enforcement's ability to investigate crimes involving mobile devices, the Secret Service opened the Cell Phone Forensic Facility at the University of Tulsa in 2008. This facility has a three-pronged mission: (1) Training Federal, State, and local law enforcement agents in embedded device forensics; (2) developing novel hardware and software solutions for extracting and analyzing digital evidence from embedded devices; and (3) applying the hardware and software solutions to support criminal investigations conducted by the Secret Service and its partner agencies. To date, investigators trained at the Cell Phone Forensic Facility have completed more than 6,500 examinations on cell phone and embedded devices Nation-wide. Secret Service agents assigned to the Tulsa facility have contributed to over 300 complex cases that have required the development of sophisticated techniques and tools to extract critical evidence.

These collaborations with academia, among others, have produced valuable innovations that have helped strengthen the cyber ecosystem and improved law enforcement's ability to investigate cyber crime. The Secret Service will continue to partner closely with academia and DHS S&T, particularly the Cyber Forensics Working Group, to support research and development of innovative tools and methods to support criminal investigations.

LEGISLATIVE ACTION TO COMBAT DATA BREACHES

While there is no single solution to prevent data breaches of U.S. customer information, legislative action could help to improve the Nation's cybersecurity, reduce

---

[10] CERT—not an acronym—conducts empirical research and analysis to develop and transition socio-technical solutions to combat insider cyber threats.

regulatory costs on U.S. companies, and strengthen law enforcement's ability to conduct effective investigations. The administration previously proposed law enforcement provisions related to computer security through a letter from OMB Director Lew to Congress on May 12, 2011, highlighting the importance of additional tools to combat emerging criminal practices. We continue to support changes like these that will keep pace with rapidly-evolving use of information technology and associated cybersecurity risks.

CONCLUSION

The Secret Service is committed to safeguarding the Nation's financial payment systems by investigating and dismantling criminal organizations involved in cyber crime. Responding to the growth in these types of crimes and the level of sophistication these criminals employ requires significant resources and greater collaboration among law enforcement and its public and private-sector partners. Accordingly, the Secret Service dedicates significant resources to improving investigative techniques, providing training for law enforcement partners, and raising public awareness. The Secret Service will continue to be innovative in its approach to cyber crime and cybersecurity and is pleased that the subcommittee recognizes the magnitude of these issues, the evolving nature of these crimes, and the importance of academic institutions, like Drexel University, in addressing these issues.

Mr. MEEHAN. I want to thank Mr. Baranoff for his testimony, and the Chairman now recognizes Mr. Quinn for your testimony.

STATEMENT OF RICHARD P. QUINN, ASSISTANT SPECIAL AGENT IN CHARGE, PHILADELPHIA FIELD OFFICE, FEDERAL BUREAU OF INVESTIGATION

Mr. QUINN. Good morning, Chairman Meehan, Ranking Member Clarke. Thank you for inviting me here today to discuss the FBI's role in cybersecurity, and for your on-going support——

Mr. MEEHAN. Special Agent, is—would you check to see if your mike is pushed on?

Mr. QUINN. Test.

Mr. MEEHAN. Just pull it closer to you, then, please.

Mr. QUINN. Got it. Very good. How is this? Very good. Well, good morning, Chairman Meehan, and Ranking Member Clarke, and Congressman Fitzpatrick. Thank you for inviting me here today to discuss the FBI's role in cybersecurity, and for your on-going support of the Bureau.

The purpose of this hearing is to discuss Federal, State, and local partnerships with private industry as it relates to cybersecurity. To that end, it is important to note that the FBI recognizes that in order to effectively combat the cyber threat, it is imperative we significantly enhance our collaboration not only with other Government entities, but with the private sector. On one hand, our Nation's companies are the primary victims of cyber intrusions, and their networks contain the evidence of countless attacks. On the other hand, the private sector is the key to defeating this threat. The private sector possesses the information, expertise, and knowledge to be a crucial partner in this endeavor.

One of the challenges in the past has been that, while private industry has provided us information about the attacks, we have not always provided information in return. It is in establishing and refining an exchange of valuable information about cybersecurity issues that will allow us to leverage the capabilities of both public and private sector in defeating cyber threats. The FBI's newly established Key Partnership Engagement Unit manages a targeted outreach program focused on building relationships with senior executives of key private-sector corporations.

Through utilizing a tiered approach, the FBI is able to prioritize our efforts to better correlate potential National security threat levels with specific critical infrastructure sectors. The Key Partnership team promotes the FBI's whole-of-Government and industry approach to cybersecurity in investigations by developing a robust information exchange platform with corporate partners. Through the FBI's Infraguard program, the FBI develops partnerships and working relationships with private sector, academic, and other public/private entity subject-matter experts. Primarily geared towards the protection of critical National infrastructure, Infraguard promotes on-going dialogue and timely communication between a current active membership base of approximately 26,000.

Infraguard members are encouraged to share information with Government that enhances its mission to prevent and address criminal and National security issues, and, through the utilization of the Guardian for Cyber program, active members are able to report cyber intrusion incidents in real time to the FBI. Infraguard members also benefit from access to robust on- and off-line learning courses, connectivity with other members and special interest groups, and relevant Government intelligence and updates that enable them to broaden threat awareness, and protect their assets.

The FBI's Cyber Initiative and Resource Fusion Unit maximizes and develops intelligence and analytical resources received from law enforcement, academia, international and critical corporate private-sector subject-matter experts to identify and combat significant actors involved in current and emerging cyber-related criminal and National security threats. CIRFU's core capabilities include a partnership with the National Cyber Forensics and Training Alliance in Pittsburgh, Pennsylvania, where the unit is co-located. NCFTA acts as a neutral platform through which the unit develops and maintains a liaison with hundreds of formal and informal working partners who share real-time threat information, best practices, and collaborate on initiatives to target and mitigate cyber threats domestically and abroad.

The FBI recognizes that industry collaboration and coordination is critical in combating cyber threats effectively. As part of our enhanced private-sector outreach, we have begun to provide partners with Classified threat briefings and other information, and tools to better help them repel intruders. Earlier this year, in coordination with the Treasury Department, we provided a Classified briefing on threats to the financial services industry to executives of more than 40 banks, who participated via secured video teleconferences in FBI offices across the country. We provided yet another Classified briefing on threats to the financial services industry in April 2014, with 100 banks participating via secure video teleconference in those FBI field offices.

Another illustration of the FBI's commitment to private-sector outreach is our increase in production of our external use products, such as the FBI liaison alert system, and private industry notification. We continue to counter the threats we face in engaging in an unprecedented level of collaboration with the United States Government, the private sector, and we are grateful for the committee's support, and look forward to continuing to work with you, and expand our partnerships, as we determine a successful course forward for the Nation to defeat our cyber adversaries. Thank you.

[The prepared statement of Mr. Quinn follows:]

PREPARED STATEMENT OF RICHARD P. QUINN

APRIL 16, 2014

Good morning Chairman Meehan and Ranking Member Clarke. I thank you for holding this hearing today and I look forward to discussing the FBI's role in cybersecurity. On behalf of the men and women of the FBI, let me begin by thanking you for your on-going support of the Bureau.

Today's FBI is a threat-focused, intelligence-driven organization. Each employee of the FBI understands that to mitigate the key threats facing our Nation, we must constantly strive to be more efficient and more effective. Just as our adversaries continue to evolve, so, too, must the FBI. We live in a time of acute and persistent terrorist, state-sponsored, and criminal threats to our National security, our economy, and our communities. These diverse threats facing our Nation and our neighborhoods underscore the complexity and breadth of the FBI's mission.

We remain focused on defending the United States against terrorism, foreign intelligence, and cyber threats; upholding and enforcing the criminal laws of the United States; protecting civil rights and civil liberties; and providing leadership and criminal justice services to Federal, State, local, and international agencies and partners.

THE CYBER THREAT & FBI RESPONSE

We face cyber threats from state-sponsored hackers, hackers for hire, global cyber syndicates, and terrorists. They seek our state secrets, our trade secrets, our technology, and our ideas—things of incredible value to all of us. They may seek to strike our critical infrastructure and our economy.

Given the scope of the cyber threat, agencies across the Federal Government are making cybersecurity a top priority. Within the FBI, we are prioritizing high-level intrusions—the biggest and most dangerous botnets, state-sponsored hackers, and global cyber syndicates. We want to predict and prevent attacks, rather than simply react after the fact.

FBI agents, analysts, and computer scientists are using technical capabilities and traditional investigative techniques—such as sources and wiretaps, surveillance, and forensics—to fight cyber crime. We are working side-by-side with our Federal, State, and local partners on Cyber Task Forces in each of our 56 field offices and through the National Cyber Investigative Joint Task Force (NCIJTF). Through our 24-hour cyber command center, CyWatch, we combine the resources of the FBI and NCIJTF, allowing us to provide connectivity to Federal cyber centers, Government agencies, FBI field offices and legal attachés, and the private sector in the event of a cyber intrusion.

We also work with the private sector through partnerships such as the Domestic Security Alliance Council, InfraGard, and the National Cyber Forensics and Training Alliance. And we are training our State and local counterparts to triage local cyber matters, so that we can focus on National security issues.

In addition, our legal attaché offices overseas work to coordinate cyber investigations and address jurisdictional hurdles and differences in the law from country to country. We are supporting partners at Interpol and The Hague as they work to establish international cyber crime centers. We continue to assess other locations to ensure that our cyber personnel are in the most appropriate locations across the globe.

We know that to be successful in the fight against cyber crime, we must continue to recruit, develop, and retain a highly-skilled workforce. To that end, we have developed a number of creative staffing programs and collaborative private-industry partnerships to ensure that over the long term we remain focused on our most vital resource—our people.

As the committee is well aware, the frequency and impact of cyber attacks on our Nation's private sector and Government networks have increased dramatically in the past decade, and are expected to continue to grow. Since 2002, the FBI has seen an 82 percent increase in the number of computer intrusion investigations.

RECENT SUCCESSES

While the FBI and our partners have had multiple recent investigative successes against the threat, we are continuing to push ourselves to respond more rapidly and prevent attacks before they occur.

One area in which we recently have had great success with our overseas partners is in targeting infrastructure we believe has been used in Distributed Denial of Service (DDOS) attacks, and preventing that infrastructure from being used for future attacks. A DDOS attack is an attack on a computer system or network that causes a loss of service to users, typically the loss of network connectivity and services by consuming the bandwidth of the victim network. Since October 2012, the FBI and the Department of Homeland Security (DHS) have released nearly 168,000 Internet Protocol addresses of computers that were believed to be infected with DDOS malware. We have released this information through Joint Indicator Bulletins (JIBs) to more than 130 countries via DHS's National Cybersecurity and Communications Integration Center (NCCIC), where our liaisons provide expert and technical advice for increased coordination and collaboration, as well as our Legal Attachés overseas.

These actions have enabled our foreign partners to take action and reduced the effectiveness of the botnets and the DDOS attacks. We are continuing to target botnets through this strategy and others.

In April 2013, the FBI Cyber Division initiated an aggressive approach to disrupt and dismantle the most significant botnets threatening the economy and National security of the United States. This initiative, named Operation Clean Slate, is the FBI's broad campaign to implement appropriate threat neutralization actions through collaboration with the private sector, DHS, and other United States Government partners, and our foreign partners. This includes law enforcement action against those responsible for the creation and use of the illegal botnets, mitigation of the botnet itself, assistance to victims, public-service announcements, and long-term efforts to improve awareness of the botnet threat through community outreach. Although each botnet is unique, Operation Clean Slate's strategic approach to this significant threat ensures a comprehensive neutralization strategy, incorporating a unified public/private response and a whole-of-Government approach to protect U.S. interests.

The impact botnets has been significant. Botnets have caused over $113 billion in losses globally, with approximately 378 million computers infected each year, equaling more than 1 million victims per day, translating to 12 victims per second.

To date, Operation Clean Slate has resulted in several successes. Working with our partners, we disrupted the Citadel Botnet. This botnet was designed to facilitate unauthorized access to computers of individuals and financial institutions to steal on-line banking credentials, credit card information, and other personally identifiable information. Citadel was responsible for the loss of over a half billion dollars. As a result of our actions, over 1,000 Citadel domains were seized, accounting for more than 11 million victim computers worldwide. In addition, working with foreign law enforcement, we arrested a major user of the malware.

Building on the success of the disruption of Citadel, in December 2013, the FBI, Europol, together with Microsoft and other industry partners, disrupted the ZeroAccess Botnet. ZeroAccess was responsible for infecting more than 2 million computers, specifically targeting search results on Google, Bing, and Yahoo search engines, and is estimated to have cost on-line advertisers $2.7 million each month.

In January 2014, Aleksandry Andreevich Panin, a Russian national, pled guilty to conspiracy to commit wire and bank fraud for his role as the primary developer and distributer of the malicious software known as "Spyeye" which infected over 1.4 million computers in the United States and abroad. Based on information received from the financial services industry, over 10,000 bank accounts have been compromised by Spyeye infections in 2013 alone. Panin's co-conspirator, Hamza Bendelladj, an Algerian national who helped Panin develop and distribute the malware, was also arrested in January 2013 in Bangkok, Thailand.

NEXT GENERATION CYBER INITIATIVE

The need to prevent attacks is a key reason the FBI has redoubled our efforts to strengthen our cyber capabilities while protecting privacy, confidentiality, and civil liberties. The FBI's Next Generation Cyber Initiative, which we launched in 2012, entails a wide range of measures, including focusing the Cyber Division on intrusions into computers and networks—as opposed to crimes committed with a computer as a modality; establishing Cyber Task Forces in each of our 56 field offices to conduct cyber intrusion investigations and respond to significant cyber incidents; hiring additional computer scientists to assist with technical investigations in the field; and expanding partnerships and collaboration at the NCIJTF.

At the NCIJTF—which serves as a coordination, integration, and information sharing center among 19 U.S. agencies and our Five Eyes partners for cyber threat investigations—we are coordinating at an unprecedented level. This coordination involves senior personnel at key agencies. NCIJTF, which is led by the FBI, now has deputy directors from the NSA, DHS, the Central Intelligence Agency, U.S. Secret Service, and U.S. Cyber Command. In the past year we have had our Five Eyes partners join us at the NCIJTF. Australia embedded a liaison officer in May 2013, the United Kingdom in July 2013, and Canada in January 2014. By developing partnerships with these and other nations, NCIJTF is working to become the international leader in synchronizing and maximizing investigations of cyber adversaries.

While we are primarily focused with our Federal partners on cyber intrusions, we are also working with our State and local law enforcement partners to identify and address gaps in the investigation and prosecution of internet fraud crimes.

Currently, the FBI's Internet Crime Complaint Center (IC3) collects reports from private industry and citizens about on-line fraud schemes, identifies emerging trends, and produces reports about them. The FBI investigates fraud schemes that are appropriate for Federal prosecution (based on factors like the amount of loss). Others are packaged together and referred to State and local law enforcement.

The FBI is also working to develop the Wellspring program in collaboration with the International Association of Chiefs of Police, the Major City Chiefs Association, and the National Sheriff's Association to enhance the internet fraud targeting packages IC3 provides to State and local law enforcement for investigation and potential prosecution. During the first phase of this program's development, IC3 worked with the Utah Department of Public Safety to develop better investigative leads for direct dissemination to State and local agencies.

Through IC3, Operation Wellspring provided Utah police 22 referral packages involving over 800 victims, from which the FBI opened 14 investigations. Additionally, another 9 investigations were opened and developed from the information provided. The following are reported loss totals:

- IC3-referred investigations = $2,135,264;
- Cyber Task Force initiated investigations = $385,630;
- Operation Wellspring/Utah Total = $2,520,894.

The FBI's newly-established Guardian for Cyber application, being developed for Cyber use by the Guardian Victim Analysis Unit (GVAU), provides a comprehensive platform that coordinates and tracks U.S. Government efforts to notify victims or targets of malicious cyber activity.

The FBI is working toward the full utilization of Guardian for Cyber across FBI, OGA's, State, local, Tribal and territorial governments (SLTT's) as well as industry partners, in order to increase awareness of vulnerabilities in infrastructure, forward understanding of cyber-related threats and facilitate a coordinated overall cyber incident response by the U.S. Government.

PRIVATE SECTOR OUTREACH

In addition to strengthening our partnerships in Government and law enforcement, we recognize that to effectively combat the cyber threat, we must significantly enhance our collaboration with the private sector. Our Nation's companies are the primary victims of cyber intrusions and their networks contain the evidence of countless attacks. In the past, industry has provided us information about attacks that have occurred, and we have investigated the attacks, but we have not always provided information back.

The FBI's newly-established Key Partnership Engagement Unit (KPEU) manages a targeted outreach program focused on building relationships with senior executives of key private-sector corporations. Through utilizing a tiered approach the FBI is able to prioritize our efforts to better correlate potential National security threat levels with specific critical infrastructure sectors.

The KPEU team promotes the FBI's Government and industry collaborative approach to cybersecurity and investigations by developing a robust information exchange platform with its corporate partners.

Through the FBI's InfraGard program, the FBI develops partnerships and working relationships with private sector, academic, and other public-private entity subject-matter experts. Primarily geared toward the protection of critical, National infrastructure, InfraGard promotes on-going dialogue and timely communication between a current active membership base of 25,863 (as of April 2014).

Members are encouraged to share information with Government that better allows Government to prevent and address criminal and National security issues.

Through the utilization of the Guardian for Cyber program, active members are able to report cyber intrusion incidents in real time to the FBI. InfraGard members also benefit from access to robust on- and off-line learning resources, connectivity with other members and special interest groups, and relevant Government intelligence and updates that enable them to broaden threat awareness and protect their assets.

The FBI's Cyber Initiative & Resource Fusion Unit (CIRFU) maximizes and develops intelligence and analytical resources received from law enforcement, academia, international, and critical corporate private-sector subject-matter experts to identify and combat significant actors involved in current and emerging cyber-related criminal and National security threats. CIRFU's core capabilities include a partnership with the National Cyber Forensics and Training Alliance (NCFTA) in Pittsburgh, Pennsylvania, where the unit is collocated. NCFTA acts as a neutral platform through which the unit develops and maintains liaison with hundreds of formal and informal working partners who share real-time threat information, best practices, and collaborate on initiatives to target and mitigate cyber threats domestically and abroad. In addition, the FBI, Small Business Administration and the National Institute of Standards and Technology (NIST) partner together to provide cybersecurity training and awareness to small business as well as citizens leveraging the FBI InfraGuard program.

The FBI recognizes that industry collaboration and coordination is critical in our combating the cyber threat effectively. As part of our enhanced private-sector outreach, we have begun to provide industry partners with Classified threat briefings and other information and tools to better help them repel intruders. Earlier this year, in coordination with the Treasury Department, we provided a Classified briefing on threats to the financial services industry to executives of more than 40 banks who participated via secure video teleconference in FBI field offices. We provided another Classified briefing on threats to the financial services industry in April 2014, with 100 banks participating. Another illustration of the FBI's commitment to private-sector outreach is our increase in production of our external use products such as the FBI Liaison Alert System (FLASH) reports and Private Industry Notifications (PINs).

CONCLUSION

In conclusion Chairman Meehan, to counter the threats we face we are engaging in an unprecedented level of collaboration within the U.S. Government, with the private sector, and with international law enforcement.

We are grateful for the committee's support and look forward to continuing to work with you and expand our partnerships as we determine a successful course forward for the Nation to defeat our cyber adversaries.

Mr. MEEHAN. Thank you, Special Agent Quinn. The Chairman now recognizes the district attorney of Delaware County, Jack Whelan.

STATEMENT OF JOHN J. "JACK" WHELAN, DISTRICT ATTORNEY, DELAWARE COUNTY, PENNSYLVANIA

Mr. WHELAN. Thank you, Chairman Meehan, Congresswoman Clarke, Congressman Fitzpatrick. Good morning. I would like to thank you for the opportunity to discuss cybersecurity, and how we can work together to better protect the identities of our Delaware County residents. It is a great opportunity for me to share a local perspective.

As the committee is well aware, identity theft is the Nation's fastest-growing crime. In law enforcement, we define cyber crime as any crime where a computer or the internet is used to commit or to conceal a crime. In Delaware County our detectives seen cyber crime first-hand in cases where identity thieves steal personal information and use it to gain access to a victim's financial resources. These thieves may steal mail, hack into computers, or even enlist employees at companies that have legitimate access to personal information. They also use e-mail or telephone scams to commit the crime, which is most often seen here in Delaware County, and it affects our most vulnerable population, our senior citizens.

With relatively little information, even low-tech, inexperienced criminals can begin opening accounts in another person's name and run up substantial charges. In one case we arrested Dorothy J. Miller of Haverford Township for stealing more than $150,000 from her employee—employer, Summers Hardwood Floors, located in Sharon Hill. After she assumed the identity of the company's owner, John Summers, who had passed away, Miller opened a credit card in his name and forged numerous checks, using his and his wife's signature. Through handwriting analysis, our detectives were able to charge Miller with multiple felony counts of theft, forgery, identity theft, and conspiracy.

In Delaware County we also see criminals using the internet to trick people into giving them money or merchandise. These scams run from the small-time bait-and-switch schemes that you might see on Craigslist to more sophisticated false websites that are set up to look like genuine websites, such as major banks.

Computers can also be used as instruments of stalking, or harassment via e-mail, or social networking sites. Targeting another vulnerable population, computers are used in crimes against our children, where the internet is used to traffic child pornography, and by predators who entice our children to meet them for sexual purposes. Dramatic increases in technology and its availability on the consumer level, coupled with a decline in cost, have given those who would exploit children a remarkable, effective, and far-reaching ability with which to do so.

To combat these crimes, detectives with the Delaware County Criminal Investigation Division, Economic Crime Unit, and the office's forensic crime lab, they investigate financial crime. The unit receives complaints from our local law enforcement agencies, the private sector, as well as the public. Financial crimes can refer to any number of nonviolent criminal offenses that involve obtaining financial gain through fraud, deceit, misrepresentation, or other forms of deception.

Financial crime is constantly evolving with the times, and is hitting new frontiers with the age of the internet. Identity theft can be committed against a single individual, corporation, or multiple victims. It may even be more complex because there can be more than one victim. Frequently the crime may not be discovered until long after it was committed. Perpetrators may not live in the same jurisdiction as the victim, and may commit the crime in several jurisdictions simultaneously, making it difficult for law enforcement to detect patterns, and the actual extent of the crime. For example, identity theft could be committed against a Delaware County resident by a perpetrator in Florida who has committed the same crime against several other victims across the State. Given all of the above, it is clear that identity theft is a crime that presents unique challenges to law enforcement to investigate and to prosecute.

The complexities of identity theft cases can slow down, or even hinder investigation because of the lack of resources available to conduct a cross-jurisdictional investigation. Evidence needed by police to solve a cyber crime is often held by the private industry, outside of the police's jurisdiction. For this reason, strong partnerships are essential to making cross-jurisdictional cooperation work. Investigation and prosecution can be very time-consuming, due to the volumes of records required to be examined, and the time required to obtain documents from banks and other financial institutions. The unit collaborates with and assists Federal, State, and local law enforcement in enforcing State, Federal, and local criminal laws relating to computer-related crime through forensic collection, recovery, processing, preservation, analysis, storage, maintenance, and the presentation of digital evidence.

As more and more people engage in on-line financial activities, such as shopping, banking, investing, bill-paying, our residents are becoming more vulnerable to sophisticated on-line identity thieves who target personal identification information. Identity theft can happen off-line too. In Delaware County we have seen low-tech, inexperienced criminals successfully open credit cards, and other financial accounts in another's name by stealing mail, personal items from a wallet, or even rummaging through trash for personal identification information.

In closing, no one, no individual, and no institution is immune from these type of crimes, and so increasing our awareness of the issue is one important function of our Economics Crime Unit. We alert the public to steps that must be taken to ensure their computers are secure, and their personal information is safe by sharing information through public service announcement videos, brochures, along with public presentations and seminars held in partnership with our financial institution, local businesses, and community partnerships. Thank you.

[The prepared statement of Mr. Whelan follows:]

PREPARED STATEMENT OF JOHN J. "JACK" WHELAN

APRIL 16, 2014

Good morning Chairman Meehan and Members of the House committee. I would like to thank you for the opportunity to discuss cybersecurity and how we can work together to better protect the identities of Delaware County residents.

As the committee is well aware, identity theft is the Nation's fastest-growing crime. In law enforcement, we define cyber crime as any crime where a computer or the internet is used to commit or conceal a crime.

In Delaware County, our detectives see cyber crime first-hand in cases when identity thieves steal personal information and use it to gain access to a victim's financial resources. These thieves may steal mail, hack into computers, or enlist employees at companies that have legitimate access to personal information. They also use e-mail or telephone scams to commit a crime, which is most often seen in crimes committed against Delaware County's most vulnerable population, our senior citizens. With relatively little information, even low-tech, inexperienced criminals can begin opening accounts in another person's name and run up substantial charges.

In one case, we arrested Dorothy J. Miller of Havertown for stealing more than $150,000 from her employer, Summers Hardwood Floors, Inc. located in Sharon Hill, PA. After assuming the identity of the company owner John Summers, who had passed away, Miller opened a credit card in his name and forged numerous checks using his and his wife's signature. Through handwriting analysis, our detectives were able to charge Miller with multiple felony counts of theft, forgery, identity theft, and conspiracy.

In Delaware County, we also see criminals using the internet to trick people into giving them money or merchandise. These scams run from the small-time bait-and-switch schemes as you might see on Craigslist, to sophisticated false websites that are set up to look like genuine websites, such as major banks. Computers can also be used as instruments of stalking or harassment via e-mail or social networking sites. Targeting another vulnerable population, computers are also used in crimes against children where the internet is used to traffic child pornography and by predators to entice our children to meet them for sexual purposes. Dramatic increases in technology and its availability on the consumer level, coupled with a decline in cost, have given those who would exploit children a remarkably effective and far-reaching ability with which to do so.

To combat these crimes, detectives with the Delaware County District Attorney's Criminal Investigation Division (CID) Economic Crime Unit and the office's forensic crime lab investigate financial crimes. The Unit receives complaints from our local law enforcement agencies, the private sector as well as the public. Financial crimes can refer to any number of nonviolent criminal offenses that involve obtaining financial gain through fraud, deceit, misrepresentation, or other forms of deception. Financial crime is constantly evolving with the times, and is hitting new frontiers with the age of the internet.

Identity theft can be committed against a single individual, corporation, or multiple victims. It may be even more complex because there can be more than one victim. Frequently, the crime may not be discovered until long after it was committed. Perpetrators may not live in the same jurisdiction as the victim and may commit the crime in several jurisdictions simultaneously, making it difficult for law enforcement to detect patterns and the actual extent of the crime. For example, identity theft could be committed against a Delaware County resident by a perpetrator in Florida who has committed the same crime against several other victims across the State. Given all of the above, it is clear that identity theft is a crime that presents unique challenges to law enforcement to investigate and prosecute.

The complexities of identity theft cases can slow down or hinder investigations because of the lack of resources available to conduct the cross-jurisdictional investigation.

Evidence needed by police to solve a cyber crime is often held by private industry outside of police's jurisdiction. For this reason, strong partnerships are essential to making cross-jurisdiction cooperation work. Investigation and prosecution can be time-consuming due to the volume of records required to be examined and the time required to obtain documents from banks and other financial institutions. The unit collaborates with and assists Federal, State, and local law enforcement in enforcing Federal, State, and local criminal laws relating to computer-related crime through forensic collection, recovery, processing, preservation, analysis, storage, maintenance, and presentation of digital evidence.

As more and more people engage in on-line financial activities such as shopping, banking, investing, and bill paying, our residents become more vulnerable to sophisticated on-line identity thieves who target personal identification information. Identity theft can happen off-line too. In Delaware County, we have seen low-tech, inexperienced criminals successfully open credit cards and other financial accounts in another's name by stealing mail, personal items such as a wallet, or even rummaging through trash for personal identification information.

In closing, no one, no individual, and no institution, is immune from these kinds of crimes. And so, increasing awareness of the issue is one important function of our Economic Crimes Unit. We alert the public to the steps they must take to ensure that their computers are secure and their personal information is safe by sharing information through PSA videos, brochures, along with public presentations and seminars held in partnership with financial institutions, local businesses, and our community partnerships.

Thank you.

Mr. MEEHAN. I want to thank the District Attorney. I thank each of the witnesses for their testimony. So I now recognize myself for 5 minutes of questions.

I am grateful for your oversight, and we are here talking today about how law enforcement can work together at the Federal and local level as well. I started by saying that we have issues with terrorism, nation-states who are using the internet as a method for, you know, global reach, but our focus here today is on the criminal side of this activity, because that is what most directly affects our communities, especially communities here, the individual who has had their identities taken, the small banker who has to deal with the implications of a fraud, like Target.

So that is where people are beginning, for the first time, to see how they are actually affected by the kinds of sophisticated schemes that we see. We have looked at four different kinds of examples that have just come to mind, most significantly the Target breach, about 110 million identities, 40 million actual identities stolen through the point of service that was—well, the service mechanisms. The key thing being there that they were able to access this entire system by going through a heating and air conditioning contract that had access to the major system. Nieman Marcus, some 350,000 victims, the University of Maryland, 300,000 alumni, and students, having significant identification taken. It is not just the, you know, the private sector, or large universities, or others. The Government itself, the South Carolina Department of Revenue, 40 million identities that have been taken.

Now, I am struck by two things, and I would like to ask you guys to talk about this. As I look back, I see, first, particularly with respect to the Nieman Marcus, some of these viruses, or other kinds of malware, had been in the systems for months before detected—before activity takes place. In fact, they suggested at Nieman Marcus for 8 months it had been in there. In addition, we have seen this with Target, that there were numerous times in which there were signs, or other kinds of things, in which there could have been opportunities to catch some of this activity before it either manifested itself, or at least manifested itself to the degree that it did. There is a suggestion that as many as 300,000 pings, so to speak, in the Nieman Marcus should have tipped somebody off to look better.

In light of that, what do we need to be doing better to be able to identify those kinds of malware and other things that are living within systems for long periods of time before they are identified, and what do we need to be doing better, along the kill chain or otherwise, to be taking advantage of the signals that do arise to be able to impact these kinds of threats before they reach the scope that they are? I conclude by saying I do appreciate that many times what we don't hear about is when you have successfully prevented some kind of remarkable thing, but I am asking you to give me your insights on that particular question. What do we need to be doing better, both with the time in there, as well as taking better advantage of the signals that are given? Mr. Baranoff.

Mr. BARANOFF. I will get it started. First I will say that we are dealing with a very——

Mr. MEEHAN. Once again, would you make sure that your microphone is on?

Mr. BARANOFF. Is that better?

Mr. MEEHAN. Yeah.

Mr. BARANOFF. Okay. We are dealing with a very sophisticated actor, organized actor. We are able to defeat very sophisticated, organized systems. That is why we encourage business to really reverse the model, in terms of where investment is. First and foremost, to response and recovery, as well as a relationship with a law enforcement agency with jurisdiction. It is extremely important that we are getting a full breadth of the landscape of what is taking place. If companies aren't reporting to us, that limits us as to the picture, threat picture.

Second, the one thing that we have found in almost every breach—actually, in every single major breach that we have investigated, there has been pre-attack behavior that has taken place. If you are able to identify those pre-attack anomalies, that will also help in the success of containing the issue. Then, obviously, continued investment and prevention, such as traditional prevention, like firewalls, proper segmentation, those help as well. But, again, the—probably the most critical element is the first piece, because it is not a matter of if, it is a matter of when you will suffer some type of breach.

Mr. MEEHAN. Yeah, I think you identified that—when we are talking about entrance into the systems, it requires, as you said, to reverse the process, to go almost down to the front end, to see the signals that are coming in, and to have some sort of shared responsibility in here. I noted at the outset this came in through a contractor, a subcontractor, that had access to a system.

But are we doing enough to make available to the small businessperson, to the local District Attorney's office, you know, to the small financial services organization who holds these, are we doing enough to both get them the kind of information that allows them to see the signal that is being shared so that they can react in time? I mean, one of the criticisms that we are hearing is this most recent act, Heartbleed. I am informed that there may have been knowledge of that for months before anybody shared that with a broader spectrum of people.

Mr. BARANOFF. There are many more—there are many vulnerabilities that exist beyond the Heartbleed Secure Socket Layer vulnerability. I think that, really, there are two parts here. First, the consumer has to take it upon themselves—the end result of a lot of these breaches is identity theft, and, unfortunately, the consumer needs to take it upon themselves to be viewing their credit reports, and to use cyber hygiene, as you mentioned in your opening statement. So I think that is of utmost importance.

Mr. MEEHAN. Now, Mr. Quinn, you see these from the global perspective. Again, as I said, oftentimes these are going back to Eastern European organizations. Certainly that is the suspicion with regard to the, you know, the—Target. What is your perspective on those questions about how we can——

Mr. QUINN. Well, Chairman, first and foremost, I concur with ASAC Baranoff on some of his suggestions. You had alluded to terrorism before, and I approach things mostly from a terrorism background. One of the things—the analogous things that we need to do is institute trip wires within the company. There are a couple of things that I see from a local level that happened. First and foremost, the consumer, or the potential victims, aren't necessarily educated about what the consequences are for some of these things. September 11 is often attributed to a failure of imagination. If I look at the cyber threat, and we haven't had a cyber equivalent of 9/11, and I hope we don't, but if I were to look at our vulnerabilities, it is a failure of imagination, but it is also a failure of appreciation, and perhaps recognition of the consequences.

I think some of the larger institutions do recognize the dangers and the consequences, but what you are talking about is what we anecdotally refer to as mom-and-pop operations. So it really breaks down at the local level to making sure that you have instituted trip wires, which is nothing more than effective outreach to them to educate them not only on the consequences and the threat itself, but prophylactic measures that they can take to guard against this. So for them, it won't become a catastrophic event.

Mr. MEEHAN. I see. When you use trip wires, now, I mean—but clearly we saw a contractor, and by all analysis this contractor was—even though there were standards within the industry, they may have not been as up-to-date in terms of practicing those standards. So that becomes sort of the Trojan horse way into the kingdom. But once in there, there were signals that were sent, both with respect to trip wires that were set off——

Mr. QUINN. Yes.

Mr. MEEHAN [continuing]. At Target that were not followed up on appropriately as they set the malware that went through all the point-of-service, you know, transactions. Then also, with knowledge that they were inside the system, to some extent, the exfiltration was a second time in which there were a number of opportunities to prevent the scope of information escaping. So where is the responsibility, not just on the local level, but are we getting too many circumstances in which, you know, people—well, there is another, you know, that is just another alarm going off. It almost sounds like false alarms, and people are not following up on them.

Mr. QUINN. It is a fair point. I can't necessarily speak to the Target investigation intimately because I am not involved in that at the National level, but what I can tell you is one of the challenges, when it comes to dealing with companies, is getting them to take—when the trip wires are tripped, to take that seriously. There has to be a shared responsibility. We in the Government do have a responsibility not only to investigate, but to the extent—try to mitigate ahead of time any of the consequences.

That said, once we do that, the potential victims share a responsibility in making sure that their security protocols are not only up-to-date, but adhered to. Because, quite frankly, from a risk management perspective, if you don't adhere to your own security protocols, or if you don't even have them in place to begin with, that is a liability. You create your own vulnerability. So I don't want to minimize what we in the Government have to do. We definitely have to educate the private sector, but we also have to convey the message to them to take this seriously, because if you don't, the consequences are catastrophic. The old saying about a stitch in time saves nine, it applies 100 percent to cybersecurity.

Mr. MEEHAN. My time has expired, and I will have some follow-up questions in what will be a second round, but at this point in time I want to turn to the Ranking Member for questions that she may have.

Ms. CLARKE. Thank you once again, Mr. Chairman, and to our expert panelists who have come today. Just wanted to sort-of back-pedal just a little to break this thing down as fundamentally as we can. Because, again, we are here at the local level, and when you look at the case scenario that the Target incident provides for us, it is a layered process that got us to that massive breach, and it didn't take all week to accomplish that.

I think that part of the challenge for a modern-day society is, how do we address it categorically? How does everyone see their responsibility, their obligations? How do we kind of connect the dots for each individual and/or entity in their particular space to be able to recognize what needs to be done to either mitigate a situation once it has occurred, or prevent it, ideally, from occurring?

I think that is part of the challenge for our society right now. You know, I—you talked about imagination, Mr. Quinn. The thing about technology is you don't have to have a whole lot of imagination. It will help you to facilitate whatever it is that you want to do, and people don't see imagination necessarily juxtaposed with intuition, right? So you intuitively—we use technology to a certain degree. You know you want to—you start here, and you know you want to go there, and you just figure out the tools for doing that. But most people don't go beyond, to use the imagination to say, well, what if? Except the bad actors, right?

So the question becomes, for the innocent one, how do we sound the alarm for them? That is part of the challenge in the physical world, as well as in the world of technology, and the use of the internet. Then we talked about there were trip wires, and there were indicators, but, you know, I have been in buildings where you will hear the emergency alarm go off, and no one budges. Particularly people who are used to being in an environment where perhaps the emergency alarm goes off, and everyone knows it just goes off. However, the practice of actually responding is where the failure comes in.

So the question becomes, from your point of view, how do we develop, and this is for the entire panel, a clearer understanding of exactly what constitutes cyber crime? You know, is there a categorical difference in what we are dealing with? It is prevalence, the levels of harm to consumers and companies, I mean, we have kind of got to get into the weeds. Because—think about just the layers in the Target scenario alone. That small contractor, who—how many people worked for that contractor, and who was the person, ultimately, you know, that slipped up, in terms of the cyber hygiene?

You know, and what are the implications for that? What are the implications for the consumer that didn't respond, though they know they shopped at Target, you know, and now, you know, they are in financial distress. How do we break this down categorically, and how can we better equip policymakers to debate this, the adequacy of Federal law? I joke about this a lot. I don't do it to demean it, but I still have colleagues with flip phones, you know, so just dealing with the ideas involved in cyber becomes almost a foreign concept. How do we break it down for people? How do we make it real, and how do we strip away these layers and make it categorical? That is my question.

Mr. BARANOFF. Should I get it started?

Ms. CLARKE. Yes.

Mr. BARANOFF. Okay. Let me just say this, just in the first quarter of this year, the Secret Service has responded Nation-wide to over 100 data breaches. Most of those companies are small and medium-sized businesses. They are not the large retailers that you hear about in the news. I read a recent statistic that stated that the average small to medium-sized business, when they suffer a data breach, will lose about $200,000. Eighty percent of those companies, within 6 months, will go out of business. Well, mitigating that statistic is extremely important to the Secret Service, which is why, as we collect cybersecurity information, we push it through our Department's NCCIC to get it out to the greater industry.

Ms. CLARKE. So, I mean, it is one thing being informed, it is one thing to find a way to get people to put this—put your recommendations into practice. Because, you know, that is a $200,000 hit, and you are not aware of what to do, or how to prevent it from happening in the future, becomes the challenge in the environment that we are talking about.

Mr. BARANOFF. Well, I think a lot of that work is done at the State and local level, quite frankly, which is why we train State and local police officers, prosecutors, and judges at our National Cyber Forensic Institute in Hoover, Alabama. A lot of those front-line officers, and judges, and prosecutors are handling the multitude and the lion's share of this work. That is what I would say on that.

Mr. QUINN. Well, in addition to what Mr. Baranoff had said, I think the key is making the consequences viscerally compelling. With other crimes, such as terrorism, you know immediately what the impact is. Had a Target store been blown up, and it was an act of terrorism, immediately people would have acted. It is making the abstract, the terabytes, and things of that sort, tangible.

So the way we approach it, and, again, I am speaking from a local level, at the Philadelphia level, is we have two mechanisms by which we do this. We have our cyber task forces, which are comprised of agents, analysts, and computer scientists, as well as other members of the Federal, State, and local law enforcement community. That in and of itself is an educational process. We take that expertise, and we try to leverage it through our Infraguard program. For instance, in Philadelphia we have roughly 1,500 members of Infraguard. In Harrisburg it is about 650. They are the gateways to both the significant and the more mom-and-pop operations, because the way we are evolving that is we are trying to break it down by sector. If we can communicate within the Infraguard program to all of the entities that potentially could be impacted, we take care of the educational component.

Now, how you—now, we are always going to be seeking to prevent, first and foremost. Mitigation is a different story, and that is something that we share across the board as a Government, and with the private sector. So that is—my answer to your question is making the abstract tangible, letting people know where it hurts them, potentially.

Mr. WHELAN. From a prosecutor's standpoint, in the local level, unfortunately, we get into situations, and I agree with Mr. Quinn, where economic crime, cyber crime, is dealt with on the court level more leniently, and I agree that we need to educate our judges as to the devastating impact of cyber crime. We typically are dealing with some serious violent cases, and judges treat those violent cases accordingly. However, in economic crime cases, they may not be as aggressively prosecuted or treated only because of the ramifications, compared to the violent crime aspect. So we are encouraging our judges—I have instructed our prosecutors in cases of this nature, to make sure that they are aggressively prosecuting, but we also deal with sentencing guidelines, which sets a standard range, a mitigated range, and an aggravated range, as to where the court should sentence in these type of cases.

We also—in addition to aggressively prosecuting the crime, we deal proactively with many of these situations by engaging in prevention, by going out to our senior citizen communities, going out to our parents, our PTAs, our Rotary clubs, and explaining to them how to be proactive in preventing themselves from being victims of identity theft, which is very important.

We periodically go to our business community and have forums in the business community. We invite guest speakers, such as our FBI—our local FBI office to come in and talk about cyber crime, and how they can better protect their business as a result of what we are seeing occurring on a National level, as well as a local level. So I think we need to continue with both the aggressive prosecution, as well as the prevention efforts.

Mr. MEEHAN. I thank the—and the Chairman now recognizes the gentleman from Bucks County, Mr. Fitzpatrick.

Mr. FITZPATRICK. I thank the Chairman again, and we really appreciate the testimony of the law enforcement, and the law enforcement perspective of the witnesses here today.

I wanted to follow up on, Agent Baranoff, something you stated, that, you know, a great majority of the security breaches, the victims are small and medium-sized businesses. We hear in the news about the significant security breaches, the retailer—Target organization, we have all heard about that. We have come to understand from news reports that many times when—could be an educational institution, or a retailer, or a merchant, is a victim of a security breach, of a cyber attack, that there is a lag time, that there is a lapse, if you will, between when that organization becomes the victim, when the incident occurs, and when they understood that it occurred.

Many times they are informed of the attack, of the victimization, by a third party. You know, could be their bank, credit institution, a financial services institution. Many times it is law enforcement informing the victim that they are, in fact, a victim. I was wondering if each of you, from your different perspectives, could comment on why you think there is that lapse. Is it that we are not identifying the security breach? What is it that Congress can do to help law enforcement, or help, perhaps, these institutions or merchants to understand quicker? Because it is one thing to become, you know, as a small business, to become a victim of a $200,000 hit, and the victims, you know, Chairman Meehan wanted to bring this down to a local perspective, is that small business in our community, the customers that rely on that business, the families, you know, of the employees who rely on that paycheck, they all become victims of that particular attack.

It is one thing that—to have that attack occur, but then to not recognize it, and have it occur perhaps many times, until somebody actually informs them. So I was wondering if you could just comment on why is it the lapse occurs, and what can we do better to speed up that realization?

Mr. BARANOFF. Well, some of the lapse may be resulting from investment by the companies. The small or medium-sized companies, it is very expensive to have the proper cyber mitigation in place.

I agree with what you stated earlier, that both the Trustwave and Verizon reports that we participate in, the most—they are two of the most widely-read data breach reports that exist today, they both have found in their studies, along with us, that a majority of the notification is made by an outside party, so the victim isn't knowing that they are being victimized as the event is taking place.

I think, again, the notification to law enforcement is paramount. We don't hear from a lot of folks, and I think that, you know, aside from the larger retailers, and the larger companies, the smaller ones are just as important. Again, it will give us a breadth of what is taking place. It also will help us empower the NCCIC, in pushing out its information to the broader industry, to include the financial services information sharing and analysis centers, as well as the multi-State ISACS. So I think that notification to law enforcement is extremely important.

In terms of deterrent, if we were to go down to the road of deterrent, we would certainly support legislation that strengthens 18 U.S. Code 1030, which is the Computer Data Breach statute, perhaps having it as a predicate to a RICO charge, which is a much stronger charge. So that type of legislation would be helpful as well.

Mr. QUINN. Thank you, Congressman. I echo my colleague's statements, but I also would point out that the delay sometimes could be a result of the companies themselves not being state-of-the-art when it comes to training, or even identify vulnerabilities or malware that is in their system. But I also think it would be, you know, disingenuous of me to say that—or to not acknowledge that some companies may be reluctant to notify law enforcement. It is that—that is where we kind of have—it is incumbent upon us, and the Federal, State, and local systems, to disabuse them of the notion that, when we come in, we are going to throw their operations into chaos, and that it is going to be a chaotic atmosphere, or something that is overly intrusive to them.

It is cliché to say that the Federal Government is here, we are here to help you, but we really do have to market ourselves in that respect, is that we are here to help you prevent, we are here to help you mitigate. We will maintain as small of a footprint as possible, and try to minimize the impact on your operations, and that is the investment that will keep you from losing out long-term.

Mr. WHELAN. Certainly, from our perspective, it is devastating to our local businesses when this occurs. We do see individuals that affects. Recently, over the last year-and-a-half, two of the three detectives that we have hired were hired as experts in computer forensics, and we are now looking at hiring more analysts, lay individuals, not sworn officers, that can assist us in dealing with the issue of cyber crime, so that when a business reacts, and when an individual is affected, we have the necessary tools to go out and address it. So it is becoming very expensive, from our level, to continue to fight, but the good news is that we have a great relationship with the FBI, and—in cases that are cross-jurisdictional, and in cases where we just need the assistance of the FBI, where—we reach out to our local Newtown Square office, and they have been very helpful for us.

Mr. FITZPATRICK. So what is your experience in Delaware County? Is it that, in most cases, law enforcement is notifying the victim, or the victim is contacting the District Attorney's office? Now, you mentioned in your testimony that many of these cases of identity theft and cyber terrorism, it is occurring in not just two jurisdictions, but across several jurisdictions, so you are dealing with many, many different law enforcement agencies. Does that add to the lag time and notification?

Mr. WHELAN. Absolutely, and that poses problems from an investigation, as well as a prosecutorial standpoint, so that does become a factor. For the most part, we are being notified, and hopefully as early as possible. Then we send our team of forensic experts in to look at the situation, make a determination as to where it originates, how it is affecting the company or the individual, and then act accordingly whether we are going to ask for additional help either on the State or Federal level, or can we locally handle it, prosecute it, investigate it to our fullest extent?

Mr. FITZPATRICK. I appreciate what you are doing. Thank you.

Mr. MEEHAN. I thank the gentleman from Bucks County. I have some follow-up—a follow-up question related to the discussion that we just had. That is a staggering statistic there that was just mentioned, that there is—$200,000 is a loss, and that oftentimes we see within months that company goes out of business. To me, that really recognizes the impact of this on a local level. We are talking about the social costs of cyber crime. We often discuss on the macro level, you never know when you didn't get the project because somebody stole your bid information before it was placed. The cyber espionage can be real, but this statistic where, you know, we have a local company, and the margins are so thin. So in addition to the financial crime, we are losing jobs associated with this. This is having a real impact.

I met yesterday with a local 501(c)(3) organization, you know, a non-profit entity, with a staggering $650,000 hit that came through a network in which their network was compromised without their knowledge. Now, insurance is going to carry about a third of that, and they may be able to litigate, but it is going to take them years to get a resolution. Meanwhile, they are on the hook for $400,000, and this is a non-profit entity. So how do we deal with financial institutions, small businesses? Where is this sweet spot? Because we are asking them to engage more in their home cyber protection, but how do they know what is the right amount? Because you could—it could be an endless process of trying to protect the fortress, so to speak.

So in line with this dynamic process, in which we pick up information at different points in time, how are we getting to the people that we know are impacted, because we know there is information from their systems, and giving them real-time information that allows them to catch up with everybody else in a timely fashion before they find themselves victimized?

Mr. BARANOFF. Well, the sharing of that cybersecurity information is probably one of the most paramount preventative methods that you can have. That is why we encourage folks to join our electronic crimes task forces, to attend our meetings. We push out cybersecurity information through our electronic crimes task forces just as quickly as we do through the FSISAC, through the Departments, NCCIC, and so on.

Mr. MEEHAN. So is the key, I mean, to work through—again, because, while you may have a local—I keep going back to banks. You know, you may have a local bank that is sizeable that, on a monthly basis, attends your meetings there, or Infraguard, but, you know, you have small community-based organizations that may have four or five branches, and how do they find the time to take somebody out once a month to, you know, spend the better part of a day getting that? Where—how do we get down—through what mechanisms do we get down to the local level to get to the people who need the information?

Mr. BARANOFF. Well, in terms of our task forces, they are regionally-based, so the issues that are affecting the Southwest are different than the issues affecting the Northeast. Those particular issues, related to the region that they are in, are addressed by that particular task force. So whether it is cybersecurity information related to the banking industry, or cybersecurity information related to the oil and gas industry, that information is shared in real time with those particular partnerships.

Mr. MEEHAN. Do we reach out to people, or do we compile lists so that we know somebody has likely had their system impacted, and do we go out, even if they are not part of an association, or part of an ISAC, or part of even a Chamber of Commerce or something? Do we go—get down to trying to let victims know that they have been victimized?

Mr. BARANOFF. We absolutely do, and one thing that we take pride in at the Secret Service is that when we call you, we have information that is actionable. We have information, you know, we know where the needle is, and what haystack to look under. That is based on the proactive nature of our investigations. We are willing to burn a source, for example, to maintain the resiliency of an organization. Prosecution for us, quite frankly, is secondary. So we do get out to the industry, and we do provide that information in real time to save that company. I can tell you last year alone we saved several small or medium-sized banks from going under because of the information that we provided.

Mr. MEEHAN. Special Agent Quinn, do you have some thoughts on that?

Mr. QUINN. I concur wholeheartedly. I mean, our mechanism is a little bit different, but it is the same principle. We utilize the Cyber Task Force and the Infraguard chapters that are within, and, quite frankly, we outsource messaging to them. We identify sector chiefs—we're in the process of identifying sector chiefs because what can happen is, and it is alluded to already, a lot of these small to medium-sized businesses may not ever know. If we get a tip, it is incumbent upon us to get out there to notify them to—important to mitigate, but also prepare them, to prevent something like that from happening again. Also share it among—across sectors in the event that it might be a continuing threat against other sectors.

Mr. MEEHAN. DA, do you—how do you perceive information being taken down to your level, with your colleagues in law enforcement, or the entities that come to you with concerns or complaints?

Mr. WHELAN. Well, certainly we have come across situations where individuals will approach us and ask us as to how they can be better protected, and what issues can they take? We certainly refer them to the resources that are available for that particular information, whether it be through the State level, or through the Bureau level, with the FBI and the Secret Service.

However, many times what we are dealing with is going out into the community through our white collar crime unit. In addition to investigating the crime, we will go out there and meet with various business entities. We will also meet with various individuals that may be vulnerable to crime, and address some of the concerns that they have, and they will relate information to them. So, from that perspective, we are proactive, but, for the most part, unfortunately, from our perspective in the prosecutor's office, we are reacting when a person already becomes a victim to a crime. But we have developed over the years many proactive programs.

Mr. MEEHAN. Thank you. I turn to the gentlelady from New York.

Ms. CLARKE. I thank you, Mr. Chairman, and, you know, we know that private-sector companies, individuals, and law enforcement efforts are complicated by the borderless nature of cyber crime. It is like—it is insidious when there is the ability to be able to tamper with the systems that exist, that are all connected to the internet. It is almost like quicksilver, because we all know that cyber criminals are not hampered by physical proximity. There can be regional, national, international borders involved. We know that they can be physically located in one nation or state, and direct their crime through computers in multiple nations or states, and store evidence of crime on computers in yet another nation or state.

So my question to you is a couple of things. No. 1: Does this beg for us to develop a new level of law enforcement and jurisprudence to address just the nature of how this operates? Is there a particular stratification that needs to develop to—so that, you know, it doesn't take the DA, you know, 2 weeks before he is able to begin an investigation, trying to capture forensic evidence that may be in his jurisdiction, but could easily be shifted? I want us to think about that picture, because I have a hard time viewing what we are dealing with right now as a society under the current boundaries of the laws that exist.

I mean, crime is crime, yes, but the nature of this one, the ability to do things so quickly, is not something that we are all accustomed to. I want to raise that with you and get your——

Mr. BARANOFF. I would agree. The international component is essential. The vast majority of our greatest threat actors in cyber are located overseas. The most sophisticated actors are overseas, attacking our infrastructure. Fortunately, the Secret Service has an outstanding relationship with some of the best cyber units located abroad, to include the Dutch National High Tech Crime Unit, the German BK, and the like. We rely on them to work with us to both capture these individuals, as well as collect evidence. A lot of the evidence ends up in overseas countries. So that international component is essential, and we need to continue to grow and expand that international presence to bring these cases to a good conclusion.

Mr. QUINN. Ranking Member, law will always lag behind technology. We see it across all programs, all investigative programs. I see it most significantly on the National security side, when it comes to new techniques, and how to accommodate—things of that sort. But like Mr. Baranoff had said, what we do—and because of that, it is—it is paramount that the relationships that you have overseas, both through—within the FBI, our FBI legal attaché network—we have roughly 64 legal attachés across the world, with 200 sub-offices.

They are crucial, because it is their relationships with their foreign government counterparts that enable us to dual—accomplish the dual objectives of attribution, which is important, but when you think about it, what is the value of attribution if you can't do anything against them? We rely heavily upon our foreign service partners to execute some type of law enforcement action against them. So until the law captures or catches up to that, we have to rely upon the personal relationships.

Mr. WHELAN. Once our cyber detectives make a determination that a crime is committed, what they will do first is try to preserve that evidence, collect it, investigate it, preserve it. Once we recognize that it has crossed jurisdictional lines, we will contact the FBI, give them the information that we have, and cooperate with the FBI with everything we can do from the local level, and work with them as a—on the National issues, based on the evidence we have already presented to them.

Ms. CLARKE. So I guess I am hearing from everyone that our current laws are sufficient for us to be able to do what we need to do in order to protect our citizenry, and address actors that may be seeking to do us harm, that we are in a place where we are not yet ready to approach these concerns in a way in which—the one thing about laws is they serve a lot of purposes. One, it is to help redress the harm that may have been done to someone, but oftentimes people see them as a deterrent to types of behaviors that, if you know what the consequences are, you know, because it is in statute or law, you are going to think twice, or you are going to understand what the implications are.

My concern is that I don't know that people actually understand the implications of a lot of what is taking place on the internet, in terms of law, and I don't know where we are going to catch up with it. In the interim, there are just some legal breaches that are happening along the way to individuals that are just using this technology, some meaning to do harm, others sort of stuck in the gray area, some kids, you know, that get on the internet and act stupid. How do we approach this now, if what we are saying is, "Well, the laws are always going to lag behind the technology"? Any ideas?

Mr. QUINN. Well, I can venture just—you—because that is—I am the one that said that the laws will always lag behind technology. Keep in mind that the value of a law is only as good as your ability to enforce it. So I think that it is going to be a whole Government approach. Our ability to enforce either our own laws, or perhaps leverage the laws of, for instance, a foreign country, where an actor is committing these type of cyber crimes, there may be a political and a—there may need to be political and diplomatic leveraging mechanisms, and so I don't want to create the impression that reliance upon the law is going to be an end-all, be-all to that.

Mr. MEEHAN. I thank the gentlelady. Before I let you go, let me just ask one other question as we are going through this, because we are talking about systems that are, you know, the systems aren't static, and how are we dealing with the changing technology? I mean now, rather than—protecting something used to be the computer system within a business. You know, we are seeing cell phones, we are seeing GPS, we are seeing skimmers that can be used, or iPads. I mean, people now have in their hand the full computing power they used to have in the heart of a business. It seems like it is getting tougher.

Mr. BARANOFF. I would say that, you know, when I first started in cyber about 7 years ago, the technology changed probably every 18 months. Today I would say it is a third of that, probably every 6 months. It is challenging for us, in that environment, to stay up with technology, certainly with the training that is needed to investigate a lot of these crimes.

Mr. QUINN. For us, you are absolutely right, it is probably one of the bigger challenges that we face. What we have to do in order to stay on the cutting edge is recruit computer scientists to come in, and that in and of itself can be a challenge, because they have opportunities that are unique, and, quite frankly, more lucrative out in the private sector. But in addition to training our own workforce, and taking responsibility for it within, we have to bring others in who have the expertise, and at the same time leverage partners in the private sector who can help us do the same things.

Mr. WHELAN. We are constantly updating, and having our detectives, our computer forensic detectives, in new trainings, new courses, new certifications. It seems like every couple months the detectives are away from the investigation, or at schools, to update themselves on the new technology. Now we are looking at hiring new analysts, and looking at new technology to bring them in so that they are coming in at a level with the current technology, as opposed to someone that has been out there that may not have been updated. So it is a constant battle, and it is a constant expense for us.

Mr. MEEHAN. Well, I thank the entire panel for your presence here today, but not just your testimony, but for your good work in these areas. As I said at the outset, we don't hear about the crimes that aren't committed, and so there are some remarkable things that are being done. I—the takeaway I get from this is the responsibility that we have to encourage businesses that aren't coming forward, those who are part of your Infraguard, to report in, those that are part of your Electronic Crimes Task Force. The—people that are coming in to your, you know, they may be dealing with you in the form of reporting something that is a local crime, but not taking the time to make sure that they share that with a—with the National matrix, because you never know where the weakest link is, and where something is coming in.

So thank you for the good work that you are doing, and I am particularly appreciative of your being here today. We will take a moment for the second panel to organize itself.

Let me thank our second panel for your patience in being with us today, and again for your testimony, or your prepared testimony. I am very grateful. You tell, and are an important voice in this dynamic. While we have spoken to law enforcement about the procedures, you are the ones on the front lines, in terms of dealing with the implications of this, or looking at the issues with respect to the totality, but particularly as it affects the victims that ultimately work through some of the entities in commerce.

So we have—we are pleased to be joined by three more panelists to conclude our hearing. The first is Mr. Ted Peters. He is the chairman and CEO of Bryn Mawr Trust. That is a company that provides personal and business banking throughout the State of Pennsylvania. Mr. Peters has more than 30 years' experience in the banking industry, including many successful entrepreneurial endeavors. He has been at the helm of Bryn Mawr Trust since 2001, and certainly has seen the growth in this area. In addition, Mr. Peters was elected to serve a 3-year term on the Federal Reserve Board, Bank of Philadelphia Board of Directors.

Joining Mr. Peters is Mr. Tom Litchford. He is the vice president of retail technologies at the National Retail Federation, and the National Retail Federation is the world's largest retail trade association, representing all varieties of retail stores across more than 45 countries, and including the Targets of the world. As vice president, he leads and manages the NRF's IT leadership community, including its Chief Information Officer Council. He also oversees the Federation's Association for Retail Technology Standards as its executive director, where he develops and enhances domestic and international relationships between retail and technology companies. Mr. Litchford, thank you for being with us.

Last, we are joined by Matthew Rhoades, who is the Director of Cyberspace and Security Programs with the Truman National Security Project, and the Center for National Policy. In this role, he leads the program's Steering Committee, and directs the organization's cybersecurity policy initiatives. Previously he served as the director of legislative affairs at the Truman National Security Project, and in that capacity he ran the Congressional Security Scholars Program, and was the principal author of the Truman Security Briefing Book. I know you enjoy an overall perspective on this, and we are looking forward to your thoughts.

So I thank you all for being here. Your written statements will appear in the record, so I look forward to your verbal testimony. Mr. Peters, the Chairman now recognizes you for your opening statement.

STATEMENT OF FREDERICK "TED" PETERS, CHAIRMAN AND CEO, BRYN MAWR TRUST

Mr. PETERS. Yes. Chairman Meehan, Chairperson, or Chairwoman Clarke, and—excuse me, Chair—Congress—Congresswoman Clarke, and Congressman Fitzpatrick, thank you for having me as a witness in this area of critical importance to our country. As a banker for almost 40 years, I will try to focus my comments and testimony on issues relating to the financial services industry and its clients. Some quick background on Bryn Mawr Trust, where we recently celebrated our 125th anniversary as a Philadelphia area institution, we are a $9.5 billion organization, with over $2 million of banking assets, and $7½ million—excuse me, $7½ billion of trust and investment assets, and we serve primarily individuals and closely-held businesses which operate in this region.

All banks and financial institutions are extremely alarmed at the actual potential threats of cyber crime. At our bank we have devoted extraordinary amounts of time, man- and women-power, and money to protect our bank, all of our clients, from this growing problem. In fact, it is approximately $1 million a year we spend on this.

In the United States and world-wide, cyber crime and cyber threats are multiplying at an alarming rate. These threats come in the form of hacking, phishing, its more sophisticated derivative spear phishing, malware intrusion, and the well-publicized DDOS, or Distributed Denial of Service, attacks, which have been perpetrated on many larger U.S. financial institutions.

Who are the bad guys? They are no longer precocious teenagers operating at 3:00 in the morning in their parents' rec rooms. Today's perpetrators are high-level professionals who fall into a number of categories. Organized crime rings are responsible for over half of all attacks. These are well-organized groups which occupy in a structured and efficient manner, with profit and loss statements much like legitimate businesses. Their sophistication is extremely high, and improving almost daily.

Next are the State-supported enterprises, which comprise about a quarter of all attacks. These enterprises have different motives than organized crimes—crime, and are usually looking for intelligence information that would give a nation-state some political or military advantage. Primary offenders here are China, and the former satellite countries of the Soviet Union.

A third group would be the hacktivists, and you have probably heard of some of these groups, such as Anonymous, or the Tunisian Hackers Team, and these organizations are usually not seeking financial gain, but are more interested in making headlines. Although hacktivists only account for a small percentage of attacks, they have very—been very successful in creating a series of high-profile DDOS attacks against financial institutions in the United States.

Last, current and former employees and vendors also provide a serious threat. I think we have all heard of a gentleman named Edward Snowden.

One of the biggest threats to banks around the country are corporate and individual account takeovers, initiated by malware being secretly installed on a business or person's computer. Again, you will recognize some of the names of his malware, Citadel, Trojan, Zeus. Once inside, the perpetrator will then move money around, and eventually try to clean out the accounts.

Point-of-sale payment systems are another favorite target of malware criminals. Once the malware is secretly installed on a merchant's computer, the malware allows cyber criminals to access all the unencrypted credit card and debit card information, and at times the encrypted data as well.

What is the solution? Unfortunately, there is no 100 percent solution. The cyber criminals who are out there always try to stay one head—one step ahead of the financial services industry. The following, however, are considered best practices to reduce the possibility of any attack being successful. First, businesses, and individuals, and financial institutions, need to use a multi-layered approach. This means a combination of many risk-based, predictive, and behavioral technologies which are out there. Companies, and consumers, and financial institutions who provide a hardened target will find the cyber criminal moving on to new and an easier victim. Next, financial institutions must build a strong feedback loop so that any intrusion can be identified, and defended accordingly. Last, we must continue to perform on-going assessments of risk, and improving our defenses.

With that, Mr. Chairman, my testimony is concluded.

[The prepared statement of Mr. Peters follows:]

PREPARED STATEMENT OF FREDERICK (TED) PETERS

APRIL 16, 2014

Thank you for having me as a witness in this area of critical importance to our country. As a banker for almost 40 years, I will try to focus my comments and testimony on issues relating to the financial services industry and its clients.

Some quick background information on the Bryn Mawr Trust Company, where I currently serve as chairman and CEO. At Bryn Mawr Trust we recently celebrated our 125th anniversary as a Philadelphia area financial institution. We are a $9.5 billion organization, with over $2 billion of banking assets and $7.5 billion of trust and investment assets under management or administration in the States of Pennsylvania and Delaware. We serve primarily individuals and closely-held businesses which operate in this region. Not only have we survived numerous wars, recessions, and depressions, but have thrived and are one of the highest-performing banks in the Nation.

All banks and financial institutions are extremely alarmed at the actual and potential threats of cyber crime. At our bank we have devoted extraordinary amounts of time, man-, and woman-power, and money to protect our bank and all of our clients from this growing problem.

In the United States and world-wide, cyber crime and cyber threats are multiplying at an alarming rate. These threats come in the form of hacking, phishing, its more sophisticated derivative spear-fishing, malware intrusion, and the well-publicized DDoS or "Distributed Denial of Service" attacks on larger U.S. financial institutions.

Who are the "bad guys"?

They are no longer precocious teenagers operating at 3 in the morning in their parents' rec rooms. Today's perpetrators are high-level professionals and fall into a number of categories.

Organized crimes-rings are responsible for over half of all attacks. These are well-organized groups which operate in a structured and efficient manner with profit-and-loss statements much like a legitimate business. Their sophistication is extremely high and improving almost daily.

Next are state-supported enterprises which comprise about a quarter of all attacks. These enterprises have different motives than organized crime and are usually looking for intelligence information that would give a nation-state some political or military advantage. Primary offenders here are China and former satellite countries of the Soviet Union such as Bulgaria, Romania, and the Ukraine.

A third group would be the "hacktivists" and you have probably heard of some of these groups such as "Anonymous" or the "Tunsian Hackers Team". These organizations are usually not seeking financial gain, but are more interested in making headlines. Although "hacktivists" only account for a small percent of attacks, they have been very successful in creating a series of high-profile DDoS against financial institutions in the United States.

And lastly, current and former employees and vendors also provide a serious threat. I think we have all heard of a gentleman named Edward Snowden.

One of the biggest threats to banks around the country are "corporate and individual account takeovers" initiated by malware being secretly installed on a business or person's computer. Again you will recognize some of the names of this malware—Citadel, Trojan, and Zeus. Once inside, the perpetrator will then move money around and eventually try to clean out the accounts.

"Point of Sale" payment systems are another target of malware criminals. Once the malware is secretly installed on a merchant's computer, the malware allows cyber criminals to access all of the unencrypted credit card and debit card information, and at times the encrypted data as well.

What is the solution? Unfortunately there is no 100% solution. The cyber criminals are out there always trying to stay one step ahead of the "good guys". The following, however, are considered "best practices;" to reduce the possibility of any attack being successful.

First, businesses and individuals need to use a multi-layered approach. This means a combination of many risk-based, predictive, and behavioral technologies which are out there. Companies and consumers who provide a "hardened target" will find the cyber criminal moving on to a new and easier possible victim.

Next, build a strong "feedback loop" so that any intrusion can be identified and defended accordingly.

And lastly, continue to perform on-going assessments of risk and improving one's defenses.

With that, Mr Chairman, my testimony is concluded.

Mr. MEEHAN. I thank you, Mr. Peters.
The Chairman now recognizes Mr. Litchford.

STATEMENT OF THOMAS LITCHFORD, VICE PRESIDENT OF RETAIL TECHNOLOGY, NATIONAL RETAIL FEDERATION

Mr. LITCHFORD. Thank you, Chairman Meehan, Ranking Member Clarke, and Representative Fitzpatrick. Thank you for giving me this opportunity to provide you with my thoughts on safeguarding consumer information from cyber attacks. Again, my name is Tom Litchford, and I am vice president for retail technologies at the NRF. In that role, I manage the CIO Council, the IT Security Council, and the Association for Retail Technology Standards, and we serve over 12,000 members around the world in the retail industry.

Regarding the recent cyber attacks, I would first like to comment on the often-forgotten fact that these breaches are perpetrated by criminals, and often they are very sophisticated criminals that are breaking the law. The targeted retailers are victims in these situations, and these victims care deeply about maintaining the confidentiality of their customer information, because if they lose that data, they lose their customers' trust, and ultimately they lose business.

The retail industry makes significant investments every year in order to protect confidential customer information. Collectively, retailers spend billions of dollars annually to safeguard data and fight fraud. But the NRF also understands that preventing cyber crime is a complex endeavor, that no single solution or silver bullet exists. Breaches still occur, and not just in the retail industry. Indeed, in 2013 more breaches happened at financial institutions than at retails stores and websites, and no industry is immune from this.

Regarding the problem here, in retail breaches, the criminal hackers want to steal consumers' payment card data, which they can easily then monetize by fencing the stolen numbers on black market websites. U.S. retailers are targeted because we not only see the greatest number of cardholders, but our merchants have to accept 50-year-old, fraud-prone payment card technology. In the United States, a signature, and a magnetic stripe with unencrypted card numbers are all that is needed to authenticate a customer and receive payment authorization. NRF supports an immediate move to replace the virtually worthless signature authentication with much more secure personal identification numbers, or PINs, as is used most everywhere else in the world. If marginally more security is needed, then a computer chip technology could be added to cards and card readers, but with significant to cost to our—all participants in the payments systems.

It is important to point out that our members', or our retailers', support for PIN and chip technology does not mean that we should be forced to adopt what is called EMV technology. EMV is a proprietary chip technology controlled by the major card brands. Indeed, EMV stands for Europay MasterCard and Visa. Worse, in the U.S. market, the EMV standard does not require a use of a PIN. The card companies require PINs in Canada, the United Kingdom, Europe, and other countries, but seek to do chips without PINs in the United States. While EMV chip without PIN certainly protects the banks, the card companies' current proposal to continue with signatures in the United States leaves the fraud door open.

Before the retail industry is expected to spend an estimated $30 billion for stores to upgrade their readers to accept partially-protected EMV cards, the NRF has urged the card networks to incorporate PINs now that focus on addressing security now so that retailers are protected, and then focus on addressing security across the entire payment ecosystem, meaning not only stores, but on-line and mobile.

In addition to addressing the problems with the current payment systems, a critical step forward is the need to foster greater collaboration. With that, the NRF believes that a heightened and well-coordinated information-sharing platform, such as a retail ISAC, is a vital component for helping retailers in their fight against cyber attacks. NRF is moving forward with the creation of such a program, that will provide retailers access to information on cybersecurity threats identified by retailers, Government, and law enforcement agencies, and partners in the financial services sector. The program, developed in consultation with the Financial Services Information Sharing and Analysis Center, the FSISAC, will launch with the establishment of an information-sharing platform for retail industry information security specialists, and plans call for a retail ISAC to be established this summer.

Recently representatives from the NRF held in-depth discussions with the United States Secret Service, and with the NCCIC, the National Cybersecurity and Communications Integration Center, and the U.S. CERC, the Computer Emergency Readiness Center, with the idea to get insight and guidance on how to improve communication, identify available resources, and collaborate more effectively to help retailers combat criminal cyber activity. NRF and its membership recognize that full robust information sharing is sometimes hampered by restrictions—legal restrictions. Accordingly, we support passage of H.R. 624, the Cyber Intelligence Sharing and Protection Act.

In conclusion, by creating a robust information-sharing platform through which retailers can better prepare themselves to defend against cyber crime, NRF is actively engaged in protecting consumer data. In supporting improved payment card technology, we seek to move the industry beyond the 50-year-old technology that makes the U.S. retail industry a prime target for these breaches. With efforts—with these efforts, as well as Congress's continued actions to encourage information sharing, we believe we can make the payment system more secure for everyone involved.

With that, thank you, and I will be happy to answer any of your questions.

[The prepared statement of Mr. Litchford follows:]

PREPARED STATEMENT OF THOMAS LITCHFORD

APRIL 16, 2014

Chairman Meehan, Ranking Member Clarke, and Members of the subcommittee, thank you for giving me this opportunity to provide you with my thoughts on safeguarding consumer information from cyber attacks. My name is Tom Litchford, and I am vice president of Retail Technologies at the National Retail Federation (NRF). In my role at the NRF, I manage the CIO Council, the IT Security Council, and the Association for Retail Technology Standards.

NRF is the world's largest retail trade association, representing discount and department stores, home goods and specialty stores, Main Street merchants, grocers, wholesalers, chain restaurants and internet retailers from the United States and more than 45 countries. Retail is the Nation's largest private-sector employer, supporting 1 in 4 U.S. jobs—42 million working Americans. Contributing $2.5 trillion to annual GDP, retail is a daily barometer for the Nation's economy.

With respect to consumer data breaches I'd first like to comment on an often forgotten fact—that these incidents have been perpetrated by criminals—and often very sophisticated criminals—that are breaking the law. The targeted retailers are victims in these situations—victims that care very deeply about maintaining the confidentiality of their customer information because if they lose that data, they lose their customers' trust, and they lose business.

Accordingly, retailers make significant investments every year in order to protect this data. Collectively, retailers spend billions of dollars annually to safeguard data and fight fraud, as well as hundreds of millions annually on PCI compliance. And yet, breaches still occur. And not just in the retail industry. You may be surprised to learn that in 2013 more breaches happened at financial institutions than at retail stores and websites. Manufacturing, transportation, and utility companies, and even professional services firms were targeted. No industry is immune.

In retail breaches, the bad actors are primarily after payment data—i.e., credit or debit card numbers—and they particularly like to target U.S. cards. Why? Because of the volume of credit and debit card numbers, and the fact that merchants must accept from customers 50-year-old payment card technology—a magnetic stripe and a signature are all that is needed to "authenticate" the customer and receive payment authorization. The bottom line is that signature and mag-stripe based cards are inherently fraud-prone products. Unfortunately, retailers and our customers are largely at the mercy of the dominant credit card companies when it comes to reducing card fraud.

So, how can we move forward? What types of solutions would reduce or eliminate the crimes of data theft and fraud?

THE WAY FORWARD TO PROTECT THE RETAIL INDUSTRY

One solution would be to replace signature authentication with an encrypted Personal Identification Number (PIN). This would greatly reduce the utility of counterfeited cards and go a long way toward reducing fraud.

Another solution that is currently receiving some attention would be to add a computer chip to the PIN and transition to the more secure "Chip and PIN" payment card technology. This technology employs a small computer chip to validate the card to the bank (i.e., confirm that it is not a counterfeit) at the Point-of-Sale (POS) terminal, in addition to requiring the cardholder to enter a PIN to prove he is the person authorized to use the bank-issued card. Chip and PIN technology dramatically reduces the value of any stolen "breached" data for in-store purchases because the payment card data is essentially rendered worthless to criminals. In addition, the PIN helps ensure that a customer and a merchant won't be defrauded even if someone steals the customer's card. This combination serves as a deterrent to breaches. The failure of U.S. card networks and banks to adopt such a system in the United

States is one reason why cyber attacks on brick-and-mortar retailers have increased domestically even as they have dropped overseas where the majority of the countries have adopted Chip and PIN payment cards.

Despite the technology's potential benefits, the Chip and PIN technology that is currently widely deployed in Europe and other developed countries, sometimes called "EMV technology," would not provide the same level of protection in the United States because, as mandated by the card brands for the U.S. market, it does not require the use of a PIN. EMV—an acronym for Europay, Mastercard and Visa—is a proprietary technology controlled by the major card brands. Further, EMV, while not necessarily violating the Durbin Amendment, currently violates the spirit of that amendment by potentially stifling the competition in the debit routing market.

No technology (and especially not EMV), is a panacea, and there is no "silver bullet" to preventing cyber crime. EMV, in particular, would take years to realize the benefit in fraud reduction. As a result, our members are exploring other means of securing data, such as encryption and tokenization. Equally important, in addition to technological changes, our members are developing measures, such as establishing information-sharing mechanisms, to address the advanced threats of the evolving cybercrime landscape.

THE VALUE OF INFORMATION SHARING

One critical aspect of next generation information security is the ability to share and receive actionable threat intelligence in a timely manner. Information sharing allows companies to better detect and defend against sophisticated cyber attacks and data security breaches. By working together and with Government to disseminate and receive cyber threat information, companies can learn where to look for signs of an attack and how to alter their security systems to "plug holes" and block attempted intrusions carried out using techniques that were effective in earlier attacks.

Importantly, third parties often possess information that can help us mitigate the risks of an attack. As the United States Secret Service (USSS) recently acknowledged in testimony before the Senate, "one of the most poorly understood facts regarding data breaches is that it is rarely the victim company that first discovers the criminal's unauthorized access to their network; rather it is law enforcement, financial institutions, or other third parties that identify and notify the likely victim company of the data breach by identifying the common point of origin of the sensitive data being trafficked in cybercrime marketplaces."[1] Victims of cyber crime can then begin to extricate fraudsters from their system and prevent further data loss when they know that an attack has taken place. Creating structures where information regarding critical threats—and certainly actual breaches—is shared swiftly can be critical in preventing and minimizing losses from data breaches.

The retail industry is in a particularly good position to both benefit from and bring value to information sharing with outside organizations and entities. Indeed, the history of data breaches affecting the retail industry indicates a pattern of increasingly sophisticated cyber attacks using similar tactics, techniques, and protocols (TTPs). During the recent spate of data breaches targeting the retail industry, the sector learned the value of such information sharing by receiving various reports and alerts from the USSS and FBI, as well as other Federal agencies (e.g., US–CERT and NCCIC) that highlighted cutting-edge TTPs. The retail industry also received valuable information from security research companies; for example, the iSightPartners report, which was disseminated through the National Cybersecurity and Communications Integration Center (NCCIC) in the wake of the Target breach, was of such particular value that NRF subsequently held a webinar for its membership where an iSightPartners' representative presented on the report's findings. In addition, in January 2014, the FBI shared a confidential report with the retail industry titled "Recent Cyber Intrusion Events Directed Toward Retail Firms" that was designed to warn the industry regarding "memory-parsing" malware that can infect POS systems. While the warnings in the report—and the findings of the iSightReport—were useful to the retail sector, NRF realized that its members would have derived significant additional benefits had they been shared sooner. It would have been more helpful had an established, trusted entity representing the retail sector existed, at the time, to receive such information in real time and disseminate it to credentialed retail business security officers.

---

[1] Testimony of Criminal Investigative Division Deputy Special Agent in Charge William Noonan, available at: *https://www.dhs.gov/news/2014/02/04/written-testimony-us-secret-service-senate-committeejudiciary-hearing-titled.*

One effective mechanism for sharing information, with a proven track record, is sector-specific Information Sharing and Analysis Centers (ISACs). In 2006, the Department of Homeland Security recommended that the Nation's critical infrastructure sectors develop ISACs to more effectively share threat intelligence. Today, the National Council of ISACs has 15 member ISACs, including 13 representing or related to critical infrastructure sectors. While the retail industry is not critical infrastructure, NRF believes that the sector could benefit from taking a similar approach to information sharing. ISACs provide a trusted source and repository for critical threat information, whether provided by outside organizations or internal members.

The Financial Services Information Sharing and Analysis Center (FS–ISAC) has been a leading example of a model that has assisted one sector in preparing for and defending against cybercrime. The FS–ISAC established various forums and tools to encourage and support information sharing among its members. Those include e-mail alerts that provide timely and actionable cyber threat intelligence, bi-weekly threat information sharing calls with security or risk management experts, as well as emergency conference calls to share particularly urgent threat intelligence. The FS–ISAC also conducts on-line webinar presentations for its members so they can share threat information and best practices. Using those tools, the financial services industry as a whole can remain aware of the most up-to-date attack prevention measures. As outlined in the next sections, NRF has already taken steps to create, or is in the planning stages of developing, similar mechanisms to encourage information sharing within the retail industry. The ultimate goal of these endeavors is to establish a robust ISAC equivalent for the retail industry. (Retail ISAC)

STEPS NRF HAS TAKEN TO CREATE A TRUSTED INFORMATION-SHARING PLATFORM

NRF already brings together senior business, technology, and loss-prevention leaders through its Chief Information Officer (CIO) Council. One subcommittee within this Council, the IT Security Council, connects information security professionals and focuses on, among other goals, promoting information sharing within the retail sector. NRF is currently using its authenticated IT Security Council email distribution list (and expanding it to also include business leaders from the CIO Council) to push out actionable threat intelligence to the retail industry. While this list currently includes only NRF members, the intention is to broaden the list, and forthcoming Retail ISAC membership, to non-NRF members as well (meaning all retailers).

Another step NRF has taken on the road to creating a Retail ISAC is to collaborate with, and learn from, the FS–ISAC. NRF has held several meetings with the FS–ISAC regarding its structure, communication methods, and policies. These meetings have allowed NRF to gain insight into how to operate an effective ISAC and avoid some of the growing pains that come with the creation of any new entity. As a result of these initial discussions, the FS–ISAC and NRF have taken steps to establish a mechanism to push out relevant critical threat information from the FS–ISAC to NRF for further distribution to its authenticated IT Security Council members. The practical experience of receiving information through an ISAC will allow NRF to better understand how information is shared in an ISAC, and what filtering is necessary to ensure that useful information is reaching the right parties.

NRF is also establishing relationships with key Government agencies. The Government collects valuable information regarding security incidents through its cyber crime investigations and broad information sharing activities. NRF has held meetings with the United States Secret Service to discuss the methods the agency currently uses to distribute critical threat information, and how the Retail ISAC could become a valued partner. Establishing a Retail ISAC will offer a quicker avenue for the USSS (and other law enforcement agencies) to share valuable information with the retail industry.

NRF has also met recently with the National Cybersecurity and Communications Integration Center to discuss how the Retail ISAC could receive actionable intelligence for its members as quickly as possible. The NCCIC is a central communications point for critical infrastructure entities, various Government agencies and international investigators where cybersecurity information is sent, analyzed, and shared with relevant parties in real time. NCCIC consists of four branches, including the U.S. Computer Emergency Readiness Team (US–CERT). These connections with the USSS and NCCIC are helping to establish an information-sharing bridge to the retail industry even as the Retail ISAC is under development.

Working with trusted advisors, NRF is currently in the planning stages with respect to a final step in the development of the Retail ISAC: The establishment of the technological and operational infrastructure to support a secure portal through which members can share information. NRF's goal is to allow credentialed members to share information of varying levels of sensitivity anonymously, thus allowing the Retail ISAC to act as a repository of critical threat, vulnerability, and incident information that is sourced from various members and outside organizations, and to facilitate peer-to-peer collaboration with the sharing of risk mitigation best practices and cybersecurity research papers. As this final step is resource-intensive and requires the active participation of its membership, NRF anticipates that it may take several months before the Retail ISAC is fully operational. In the mean time, NRF has, and will continue to, provide mechanisms and tools for information sharing among the retail industry, as outlined above.

As a final note on information sharing, NRF and its membership recognize that full, robust information sharing is sometimes hampered by legal restrictions. Accordingly, NRF supports the passage by Congress of the bipartisan "Cyber Intelligence Sharing and Protection Act" (H.R. 624) so that the commercial sector can lawfully share information about cyber threats in real time, thereby enabling companies to defend their own networks as quickly as possible from cyber attacks that are detected by other businesses.

CONCLUSION

In closing, there are three important policies that NRF supports.

First, the members of NRF support replacing today's fraud-prone mag-stripe and signature cards with cards using PINs or open-standard "Chip and PIN" technology. NRF also supports efforts to develop and deploy end-to-end encryption or tokenization, but is opposed to the adoption of "EMV" technology as mandated for the U.S. market, as it presently would not require PIN-authentication of card-holders and rely instead on simply a signature to authenticate the consumer.

Second, NRF supports information sharing within its membership and the retail industry about cyber threats and has already taken several steps to create a Retail ISAC, and continues to actively engage in making that goal a reality. A retail-focused ISAC will allow the industry as a whole to benefit from the information sharing that is so critical to effectively combat today's evolving cyber threat.

Third, we support passage by Congress of the bipartisan "Cyber Intelligence Sharing and Protection Act" (H.R. 624) legislation that will facilitate the sharing of cyber threat information in real time, thereby enabling companies to better defend their own networks based on critical information about attacks on other businesses.

Thank you for your time today. I'd welcome your questions.

Mr. MEEHAN. Thank you, Mr. Litchford.

The Chairman now recognizes Mr. Rhoades for his testimony.

STATEMENT OF MATTHEW RHOADES, DIRECTOR, CYBER-SPACE AND SECURITY PROGRAM, TRUMAN NATIONAL SECU-RITY PROJECT AND CENTER FOR NATIONAL POLICY

Mr. RHOADES. Chairman Meehan, Ranking Member Clarke, Congressman Fitzpatrick, thank you for having me here today. Information networks provide hope to millions of people around the world by creating the conditions for innovation and human prosperity to flourish, while enabling America's mutually-supportive ideals of human rights, freedom, and opportunity. Unfortunately, they are also exploited by a variety of actors to further nefarious national, criminal, and ideological objectives.

Frequently these groups, hacktivists, terrorists, criminals, and nation-states also overlap, working together towards complimentary interests, while utilizing the inherent anonymity of cyberspace. In short, today's technologies provide an unprecedented opportunity for humans to reach their full potential, while simultaneously increasing individual and collective security risks. These are facts that the Members of this committee know well, but they are worth mentioning here today because in cyber space, the difference between espionage, crime, and attacks can be as simple as intent, or just a few keystrokes.

Gaining and maintaining access to a network are the most difficult phases of a cyber incident, but once you are in a network, whether you spy, steal, or destroy is often a matter of choice. Criminals are developing new tools that are more sophisticated and more intuitive than previous generations, and then selling them in on-line marketplaces. This is lowering the barrier to entry, and giving more actors the capability to threaten critical systems. Cyber crime, in this way, is connected to both National security, and the protection of private information, and no single entity, whether Government or business, can secure a domain that extends beyond traditional geographic boundaries. Cybersecurity is a shared responsibility.

To ensure our Nation is safe, the Government must coordinate the protection of our country's most critical assets, while law enforcement agencies impose the criminal laws of the United States. Governments must also find ways to cooperate with one another on investigations. Cyber crimes are often intentionally routed through multiple countries, particularly those who provide sanctuaries against international investigations. More must be done in the international arena to build the capacity of sanctuary states, and to discourage others that are complicit in criminal activities.

Private companies must do their part as well. But in sectors where there is no choice in the consumer market, the Government should play a larger role in ensuring the security of critical networks. Many companies are collecting, storing, and analyzing information on U.S. citizens. Securing those networks, protecting our information, both require the private sector to take better responsibility for their own security.

While information-sharing programs do not offer a cybersecurity panacea, they can contribute to collective security by creating a fuller picture of the threat environment. That said, there is a right way to share information, and a wrong way to share information. All irrelevant personally identifiable information should be removed before the information is given to the Federal Government, or to other private actors. Information coming into the Federal Government should have previously-defined acceptable uses, and be given to a civilian agency, and those who participate in information-sharing programs and exhibit negligent behavior should be held responsible. Getting this right matters. The way we build our domestic programs will have privacy and civil liberties implications for Americans here at home, but also for human rights activists and dissidents abroad.

The unfortunate reality of cyber is that, given enough time, resources, sophistication, and motivation, an attacker will gain access to a network. As people become more dependent upon technology, the opportunities for crime, espionage, and physical disruption will increase. But by implementing commonly-held best practices, we can protect the great majority of our networks, secure our personal information, and allow our security agencies to focus on preventing attacks to critical systems.

Thank you for the opportunity to join you today, and I look forward to your questions.

[The prepared statement of Mr. Rhoades follows:]

PREPARED STATEMENT OF MATTHEW RHOADES

APRIL 16, 2014

Chairman Meehan, Ranking Member Clarke, Members of the committee: Thank you for inviting me to appear today to discuss how the public and private sectors can work together to increase cybersecurity.

Currently, I serve as the director of the Cyberspace and Security Program at the Truman National Security Project and Center for National Policy. Together, these two organizations represent more than 1,300 members with an expertise in numerous security issues—including cybersecurity—and a dedication to forging strong, smart, and principled National security policy for America.

The rapid development of information networks over the past 30 years has allowed individuals and nations to grow and prosper. Today, our small businesses are global enterprises—reaching markets and customers on the other side of the world with the click of a mouse. The internet invigorates economic progress and helps people rise out of a cycle of poverty in the developing world.

These tools also enable the expansion of America's mutually supportive ideals: Human rights, freedom, and opportunity. Using the internet, democracy activists in nations ruled by oppressive regimes can organize to petition for their fundamental rights; vulnerable populations in conflict-ravaged areas can show the world the brutality of their own governments; and individuals can seek out new ideas to challenge their own beliefs.

New technologies are providing hope to millions by creating the conditions for innovation and human prosperity to flourish. Unfortunately, they are also being exploited by a variety of actors to further nefarious national, criminal, and ideological objectives.

Hacktivists—or on-line demonstrators—use information networks to target opponents and draw attention to a political cause. Terrorists use information networks to spread their propaganda and recruit others to help commit acts of violence. Criminal organizations use the internet to steal from individuals and organizations all over the world and turn another's loss into their financial gain. Finally, nation-states leverage these capabilities to spy on, steal from, and potentially attack their adversaries.

Frequently, these groups—hacktivists, terrorists, criminal organizations, and nation-states—also overlap, working together towards complimentary interests while utilizing the inherent anonymity of cyber space to make attribution even more difficult.

With each new day, the number of actors with access to these tools increases and, as a result, so does the number of potential victims. Roughly 90% of the world's data has been generated in the last 2 years.[1] As more information is generated, confidentiality and privacy grow more vulnerable. Governments are losing once closely-held state secrets; companies are finding their intellectual property suddenly in the hands of competitors on the other side of the world; and individuals are losing control over their private information.

According to Symantec's "Internet Security Threat Report 2014," the number of breaches increased by 62% in 2013 with a total of over 552 million identities compromised.[2] Additionally, targeted attacks grew by 91% and are increasingly aimed at small businesses.[3]

And as we are all aware, the recent, highly-publicized breach at Target—the second-largest retailer in the United States—compromised personal information on 70 million customers by using software that may have cost less than $2,500 at an online marketplace.[4] Today, cyber criminals can use relatively easy-to-find software to make outsized gains.

The Target example shows that even the largest companies with vast resources are vulnerable. Frequently, they are unaware that a breach has even occurred. One security provider recently announced that in 2013 the median number of days attackers were present in a network prior to discovery was 229 days. That is actually 14 days less than the 2012 median.[5]

---

[1] Science Daily, "Big Data, for better or worse: 90% of world's data generated over last two years," 22 May 2013, *http://www.sciencedaily.com/releases/2013/05/130522085217.htm.*

[2] Symantec Corporation, *Internet Security Threat Report 2014; Volume 19,* p. 5.

[3] Ibid, p. 5 & p. 18.

[4] Chris Smith, "Expert who first revealed massive Target breach tells us how it happened," 16 January 2004, *http://bgr.com/2014/01/16/how-was-target-hacked/.*

[5] Mandiant, *MTrends: Beyond the Breach,* p.1.

In short, today's technologies provide an unprecedented opportunity for humans to reach their full potential while simultaneously increasing individual and collective security risks.

These are facts that the Members of this committee know well, and they are broader than the scope of this hearing. But they are worth mentioning in this context because in cyber space, the difference between espionage, crime, and attack can be as simple as intent, or just a few keystrokes.

Gaining and maintaining access to a network are the most difficult phases of a cyber incident. Adversaries spend a great amount of time, energy, and resources to seek out and secure vulnerabilities that provide access. But once they are in the network, whether they spy, steal, or destroy is a matter of choice.

Furthermore, criminals are developing new tools that are more sophisticated and more intuitive than previous generations, and then selling them in on-line marketplaces. This reality is lowering the barriers to network entry and giving more malicious actors the capability to threaten critical systems, in both the private and public sectors.

Cyber crime, therefore, is linked to National security and the protection of private information. All of the actors using cyber space for illegitimate means need vulnerabilities to exploit, and no single entity—whether Government or business—can secure a domain that extends beyond traditional geographic boundaries. In cyber space, one weak link can compromise the security of the entire system. Cybersecurity is a shared responsibility.

To ensure our Nation is safe, the Government must coordinate the protection of our country's most critical assets against sophisticated, destructive attacks while law enforcement agencies impose the criminal laws of the United States in the cyber domain. Through the development of new tools and the continued maturation of the National Cybersecurity and Communications Integration Center (NCCIC), the Department of Homeland Security (DHS) is addressing this responsibility.

But more can be done. For example, the effectiveness of the NCCIC is directly tied to the level of participation by other Federal agencies. Yet, those agencies are not currently required to share information with DHS. If we are going to task DHS with the responsibility for leading the protection of Federal civilian agencies, then we must give them the authorities required to be successful.

Governments must also find ways to cooperate with one another on investigations. Cyber crimes are often intentionally routed through multiple countries, particularly those who provide sanctuaries against international investigations. When an investigation leads to a new jurisdiction, the investigators are suddenly at the mercy of another government. More must be done in the international arena to build the capacity of nations that do not want to be criminal sanctuaries and to discourage others that are complicit in criminal activities originating in their territory.[6]

Private companies must do their part as well. Most of this country's critical infrastructure is privately-owned and operated, but market forces alone have yet to incentivize broad-scale use of cyber risk management strategies. Many companies are working to protect their networks, but too many are not doing enough. And in sectors where there is no choice in the consumer market—where a public good is being provided by a private actor—the Government should play a larger role in ensuring the security of critical networks.

Additionally, many companies are collecting, storing, and analyzing information on U.S. citizens. This information deciphers everything from our travel habits to our personal interests. Securing our most important networks and protecting our personal information requires the private sector to take better responsibility for their own security.

Finally, individuals have to take responsibility for our on-line behavior as well. Although there are sophisticated hackers at work, most compromises take advantage of existing vulnerabilities that have not been patched but could have been. The more hardened a target becomes, the more likely a hacker will look for a less secure, peripheral target as a means to get in. This is likely the reason that targeted attacks are increasingly focused on small businesses. We must contribute to a culture of security that is respectful of the rights of others, while contributing to the security of the whole system.

Universities across the country, including Drexel University here in Philadelphia, are developing educational programs to ensure the next generation is prepared to combat cybersecurity threats. These are important initiatives that warrant support. However, it will take a generation for them to fully bear fruit. More also needs to

---

[6] Richard A. Clarke, *Securing Cyberspace Through International Norms: Recommendations for Policymakers and the Private Sector*, Good Harbor Risk Management, LLC, p. 23.

be done to make today's users aware of the risks associated with their on-line behavior.

Getting this model of collaborative security correct is dependent upon trust. Governments and private entities must work together to mitigate threats. Both, however, are collecting vast quantities of information on individuals. The more information they store in their databases, the more attractive those databases become to criminals. What they share and how they share has serious privacy and civil liberties consequences for individual consumers.

While information-sharing programs do not offer a cybersecurity panacea, they can contribute to collective security by creating a fuller picture of the threat landscape. That said, there is a right way to share information and a wrong way to share information. All irrelevant personally identifiable information should be removed before the information is given to the Federal Government or another private actor. Information coming into the Federal Government should have previously-defined acceptable uses and be given to a civilian agency. And those who participate in the program and exhibit negligent behavior should be held responsible. Getting this right matters: The way we build our domestic programs will have privacy and civil liberties consequences for Americans and for human rights activists and dissidents overseas.

The reality is that given enough time, resources, sophistication, and motivation, an attacker will gain access to a network. And as people become more dependent upon technology, the opportunities for crime, espionage, and physical disruption will only increase. But with collaboration built upon trust, I believe we can reduce our vulnerabilities. By implementing commonly-held best practices, we can protect the great majority of our networks, secure our personal information, and allow our security agencies to focus on preventing sophisticated attacks against our most critical networks. And, in the end, we can more fully realize the potential of new technologies to expand freedom and opportunity at home and abroad.

Thank you for the opportunity to join you today, I look forward to answering any of your questions.

Mr. MEEHAN. I thank each of the panelists for your testimony, and your full written statements will become part of the record, so I now recognize myself for 5 minutes of questioning.

Mr. Peters, thank you for taking the time to be here with us today, representing not only your bank, but many smaller to midsized institutions as well. I was struck by the figure that you gave me, a million dollars that you are spending at a relatively sophisticated bank in and of itself, but relatively, you know, smaller, compared to the big New Yorks, or—that is a million dollars off the bottom line. That is a lot of investment. Can you tell me how you are using that kind of an investment, and how you make the choices about where to, you know, put those kinds of decisions about what you use, and what you rely on to come from other places?

Mr. PETERS. Well, a lot of it, Mr. Meehan, is a risk-reward type thing. We spend a million dollars. We could probably spend two or three if we wanted to. It goes really basically for software. I mentioned multi-level protection. That is the most important thing, is you have three or four different layers, and they all look at things differently, and that will kind-of catch things. We use a lot of outside vendors who come in and do intrusion tests on us. We have 19 people in our IT department, whatever—and it sort of points up a point which Mr. Fitzpatrick brought up a second ago, about—how about small banks, or how about small businesses? That is really, you know, we are fortunate we are large enough—we spend a million dollars, and we can afford to spend it. But you get a bank that is a $3- or $400 million bank, or you get a small business with 25 or 50 employees, they have a lot of trouble spending that type of money for this, and I think that is really one of the real challenges which we have going forward.

We do not see, by the way, that decreasing going forward. If we are—we spent a million dollars last year. We probably spent $800,000 the year before, and I think this year the budget is a $1.2 million or $1.3 million. So we are going to see this continue to escalate.

Mr. MEEHAN. Now, do you issue credit cards and other things out of your institution?

Mr. PETERS. We do not issue a credit card. Banks our size usually don't. There are usually five or six large banks in the country that issue them. However, we do issue debit cards, and, of course, they get compromised. On the Target situation that happened, we had to replace over 1,000 cards, and to, once again, Mr. Fitzpatrick—accommodation cost us $5 or $6 to replace that card. Everybody has to be personally called. They have to come into the bank personally to replace it, and there is a lot of inconvenience and time. We get no—absolutely no compensation for that at all, and this happens many, many times during the year.

But we see—very frequently we see compromised debit cards. It could—Target is obviously the most visible one, but there have been lots of other little ones around that we get reports on once a month. You know, your—at least 50 cards have been compromised.

Mr. MEEHAN. I think that is one of the points that is made, is, notwithstanding that sometimes a lot of identities are taken, that the—turning that into some sort of a compromised situation still takes a few more steps. So a lot of names are sold, but then we see phishing, and other kinds of things that take place to try to get that identity to themselves do something that allows them to be further compromised. Isn't that right, Mr. Litchford?

Mr. LITCHFORD. Right. Well, I—and I think the previous panel addressed the fact that consumers need to be educated too, and to protect their sensitive data. But, at the same time, in terms of the retail breaches, the data that they are getting alone is not enough for identity theft. It is primarily the card numbers that they are after. What the bad actors do is then, in turn, sell those numbers in bulk. As you know, with the current technology of those cards, it is very easy to then go make a counterfeit card. Because we are using signature as the second form of authentication, it is very easy for them then to go commit fraud with those numbers.

So the costs here are on the banks and the retailer side. At most, the consumers are probably inconvenienced. I mean, I, for one, was part of the Target breach, and Chase replaced my card, and I had to go through and update my auto payments, and things like that. So it was more of an inconvenience at the consumer level, but the cost of that fraud is being borne by the commercial businesses, such as banks and retailers.

Mr. MEEHAN. Now, you have also mentioned the idea of the technology, 50-year-old technology. What is the solution with respect to the cards? You mentioned what is happening in Europe, but that isn't a preferred solution for you. What is the——

Mr. LITCHFORD. Right.

Mr. MEEHAN [continuing]. Solution?

Mr. LITCHFORD. I think there are a couple things. I mean, first, you know, just back to EMV, to understand, EMV was created over 20 years ago to address a problem outside of the United States that was not a particular issue in the United States. When that technology was developed, it had no inkling of this thing called the internet, or e-commerce, or now what is called emerging mobile commerce, with mobile payments. So that technology is designed to only stop counterfeit cards predominantly. Or if I were to lose the card, and you were to pick that card up and try to use it, it would stop that, because it has a PIN on it, right?

So with that, if the cost to implement that type of technology in the United States, which we anticipate on the retailer side alone is over $30 billion——

Mr. MEEHAN. Why so much?

Mr. LITCHFORD. Because of the cost of replacing the equipment and software, and training at the stores. There is—again, the cost is anticipated to be anywhere from, I think, $500 to $1,500 per lane. So when you are in a retailer, they are having to replace not just the hardware, but train their people how to use it, replace the software that handle the systems, and things like that.

So, again, we just believe that that money could be better spent addressing the entire ecosystem, not just part—present situations, such as in stores, but also to start looking at——

Mr. MEEHAN. Well, what is the entire situation? Because as you are speaking, I am considering the idea. I am thinking——

Mr. LITCHFORD. Yeah.

Mr. MEEHAN [continuing]. In the one sense, why wouldn't we be moving forward into newer technology? But, at the same time, if you are spending $30 billion to do this, the dynamic nature of—are they going to find some other way to get into the middle of that transaction, so it is not done at the counter, but it is done some other——

Mr. LITCHFORD. Right.

Mr. MEEHAN [continuing]. Part——

Mr. LITCHFORD. So EMV, as a technology, the card number is still in the clear, just so you know. The encrypted portion of EMV is just to validate that the card is the real deal, this is not a counterfeit card. So we could still potentially see those—they are called PANs, or personal account numbers, exposed, and then used to do transactions in other environments, such as on-line or mobile. Which is where, frankly, the industry or—and consumers are going.

So, you know, even where EMV has been deployed, you know, we are quick to tout, yes, we have stopped all this fraud in our stores, but we have moved the equal percentage to on-line environments, so the fraudsters will go to where they can easily monetize the data. So, from a retailer's perspective, what we want to do is—we know this cyber war we are in is a war that is going to be a continual war. The goal is not necessarily to stop breaches, but to stop their ability to monetize any data that they would get from that breach.

So retailers are already taking steps now to try to eliminate any of that sensitive data within their systems. As an example, I am already seeing many retailers start to invest in significant cost into something called encryption and tokenization. So once I swipe my card at the retailer's terminals, it is immediately encrypted, so that that number is no longer in the clear. Of course, we have to work with financial institutions to handle things like that, as well as tokenization.

So, again, you know, I think the money—another thing you can do, by the way, is, on your current mag stripe card, is you could simply put a PIN on that today, and that would have probably stopped most of the fraud that is occurring in the United States. So, again, our position is we would like to see the entire payment ecosystem addressed, not just focus on a particular piece of that. Even then the focus is on—at least what the cards are pushing down on retailers is not even to have PINs. They want to just put a chipped card out there, and still allow you to use your signature for that. So we think that is not a full solution.

Mr. MEEHAN. Well, I thank you. My time is expired, and I will turn to the gentlelady from New York.

Ms. CLARKE. I thank you, Mr. Chairman. I want to also thank our expert panelists, and say—and respond to Mr. Peters, and your earliest salutation to me, that hope springs eternal.

Mr. PETERS. Right.

Ms. CLARKE. The private sector's focus is on the development and implementation of technology systems to protect computer intrusions and malicious code, internet fraud, spam, and if a crime does occur, to detect it, and gather admissible evidence for an investigation. The private entities that focus on these technological efforts include internet service providers, security vendors, software developers, and computer forensic vendors.

Internet service providers offer businesses and home users various levels of access to the internet, and other internet-related services, such as customer support, and spam and virus protection. Providers also assist law enforcement by monitoring and providing information on selected internet activities, and provide technical expertise.

How does a company who employs the services of security vendors decide when to report a cyber crime, and when to allow or encourage its security vendors to cooperate with law enforcement in the investigation and prosecution of a cyber crime? Can you give a sense of, you know, how does it all come together, and, you know, what is that moment where it sort of says, eureka, let us move in this immediately, because it is me now, it could be someone else in the next——

Mr. PETERS. If I could start? Yeah, first of all, we report everything. We are required, as a financial institution, to file something called suspicious activity reports, SARs, with the Federal Government anytime anything happens. It could be somebody who is trying to launder cash through a teller, but in many cases now, actually, it is computer fraud. There is identity theft. I think last year we stopped 14 cases of identity theft at our bank. Unfortunately, one did get through. On the other hand, we get 30 attacks a night, 30 attacks in our computer system a night. Most of them are from China.

So we actually report everything to the Federal Government. We are required to do that, and we do that, and to local law enforcement. If something has identity theft, we will go to the local authorities, usually our township folks, and report that to the police department.

Mr. LITCHFORD. Yes. So, again, in retail, the predominant data that these bad actors are going after is credit card information, and many times it is not the retailer that knows that the—that a crime is occurring. It is typically, for example, our financial institution friends that have pretty decent algorithms for what is going on with fraud, that they are able to then, for example, call a retailer and say, we suspect something is going on. Then at that time—I am—can't speak for all retailers, but I assume that the law enforcement is then engaged.

One of the problems that we have in retail is the myriad of laws that they have to abide by, not only in the United States. I believe it, and I hope I get the numbers right, I think it is 47 States, plus the District of Columbia, have different uniform breach notification laws. So one of the—so you can imagine now what a retailer is trying to go through to figure out, you know, how do I respond to this State versus that State. Then—so part of the thing—things our members, and NRF, is for is a uniform breach notification law.

Ms. CLARKE. That is interesting. I had no idea that it was based on the States how you go about reporting. Very well.

Mr. LITCHFORD. Right.

Ms. CLARKE. Then, when you think about the fact that many retailers are also international now, it adds another layer of——

Mr. LITCHFORD. Yes.

Ms. CLARKE. Challenge.

Mr. LITCHFORD. Yes.

Ms. CLARKE. I wanted to just revisit with you a moment the whole idea of chip and PIN.

Mr. LITCHFORD. Um-hum.

Ms. CLARKE. It is a global standard, and we seem to be the outlier, as the United States. As you have spoken about your thinking around it, you talked about the idea of the mobile and the online——

Mr. LITCHFORD. Um-hum.

Ms. CLARKE [continuing]. Purchasing, particularly when it comes to retail items. How does that impact on our industry, the fact that we are outliers with the swipe and signature, versus the chip and PIN?

Mr. LITCHFORD. Right.

Ms. CLARKE [continuing]. You give us a better sense of that?

Mr. LITCHFORD. Well, I think the obvious impact is the bad actors have come to the United States to get that data now, because it is a place that is green pastures for them, and then they can breach systems, get the data, and then easily monetize it. So, again, the challenge here is what can we do with the current mag stripe technology to try to reduce some of the fraud that does occur when the data is breached? So I could simply put a PIN on a mag stripe today, and pretty much stop a lot of the fraud that is going on, because even if they made a counterfeit card, they would not necessarily have the PIN that goes with that card.

The other issues, you know, with EMV, again, is they are proposing in the United States not to—they are calling it chip and signature, or chip and choice, which everywhere else in the world is chip and PIN. So we are wondering what—why do you not want a PIN? What is the problem here? We know PINs are the way to safeguard things, whether it is on a mag stripe or a chip card.

Then a further potential issue we have with EMV is it is a proprietary standard, meaning it was developed by the cards themselves. With that, today, retailers, there are two rails, so to speak, that you go over for your authentication, or your authorization. One would be—what—you might think is the credit rail, and the other is the debit rail. What is really going on behind the scenes is you have a signature authorization, or a PIN authorization. When that transaction is a PIN authorization, retailers today have choice of about 18 different providers that they can go to, based on the fees that are going to be charged to them for that authorization. EMV does away with that. The debit routing is determined by the card itself, therefore, by the issuer, not the retailers.

Ms. CLARKE. That is interesting. Is there an advantage to being in a separate system all to ourselves, in terms of these retail transactions? In other words, that is driven by the card, versus, I don't know, the public, or the——

Mr. LITCHFORD. Right.

Ms. CLARKE [continuing]. Retailers, or—I mean, when you think about the fact that everywhere else, you know, for the most part, we are dealing with chip and PIN. Is there an advantage to us maintaining our own uniqueness, if you——

Mr. LITCHFORD. Right. Well, and keep in mind, at the time of EMV, the United States was far along, and well ahead, in the sophistication of our payment networks, versus the rest of the world. Today, keep in mind, if you see an EMV card from somewhere else in the world, or even many U.S. cardholders have EMV cards because they travel internationally, if you look on the back, it still has a mag stripe on it, right?

Going forward, even if we were to pursue that technology in the United States for at least 5 years or so, those cards are still going to have mag stripes on the back of them for transitional purposes. So I am not going to see benefit from Day 1 of deploying EMV technology. That is why I made the comment that you could put PINs on credit—on mag stripe cards today and pretty much immediately see an impact, not having to wait for this transitional period, and then use those investment dollars to address the entire payment ecosystem, not just what we call a card present, or in-store transaction.

Ms. CLARKE. Thank you. Mr. Chairman, I thank you for your indulgence, and yield back.

Mr. MEEHAN. I thank the gentlelady. Turn to Mr. Fitzpatrick, from Bucks County.

Mr. FITZPATRICK. Mr. Litchford, isn't one of the issues with this chip and PIN, or chip and choice, the—in terms of economies and scale, and smaller merchants, the cost of new technology requirements and terminals?

Mr. LITCHFORD. Um-hum.

Mr. FITZPATRICK. Can you elaborate on that?

Mr. LITCHFORD. Well, again, we have estimated the cost to be, you know, somewhere in the lines of $600 to $1,500 per terminal on the retailer side to deploy the ability to accept EMV cards. Is that the question? Again, that is just in retailers, right? So keep in mind, if we deploy EMV technology, there are many, many other types of businesses that take credit cards that will also have to upgrade their infrastructures, as well as the financial institutions themselves. They have all the ATMs out there that they need to replace. So there are just huge and significant costs involved.

Mr. FITZPATRICK. So retailers just consider it cost of doing business, part of the security costs going forward? But should there be a recognition on the difference between a large-scale retailer, like Target, versus a smaller mom-and-pop operation?

Mr. LITCHFORD. I am not sure what you are asking there. I mean, the cost is the cost. I think when you look at the retailers, the larger ones, like Walmart, for example, are already ready for EMV, predominantly because they are a global retailer, and they use standardized deployment of POS systems. So whatever they deploy to the United Kingdom gets deployed to the United States, so therefore they are already ready for EMV.

Mr. FITZPATRICK. Back to your previous testimony, I think what you said is that we need to recognize that, in the future, there will be cyber attacks, and some of those attacks will be successful, but the real key is trying to determine the best way to minimize the damage, and precluding any monetizing of that information in the future.

Mr. LITCHFORD. Right.

Mr. FITZPATRICK. It has now been 5 months since the successful attacks on the Target operation. What have we learned, and what have we changed, as a Nation, in those 5 months?

Mr. LITCHFORD. Um-hum. Well, again, I think one of the biggest things that, from the retail perspective, we are calling for is the lack of information, and the lack of critical information getting to us relatively speedy. As an example, from the Target breach itself, the first data that we had that we could disseminate to our members was January 16. In the mean time, we know, through these ISACs, that data was being exchanged. But my members were calling, you know, what can I do? How do I know that I have not got the same malware problem?

As soon as we got that data, NRF did a webinar with Eyesight Partners, who was one of the publishers of the paper, to our members, and walked them through. This was a very technical call. These are the signatures you need to look for, these are the DLLs you need to look for. But, again, that was a month after Target was announced, right? So one of the things, based on that learning, that we are moving forward with is this establishment of a retail ISAC.

So even though retail is not identified as a critical infrastructure, we are going to go ahead and develop this ISAC. We are working with financial services ISAC, the Secret Service, NCCICS, and U.S. CERC to make sure that we get this up and running. In the mean time, we are establishing a listserv to push data out one way. As soon as that is up, which we expect to be in the next week or so, that will then be immediately fed with TLP White and TLP Green alerts. Are you familiar with the traffic light protocol? So green is information that is shareable to the public—or white is to the public, green is to the community. But the amber and red alerts I am not able to push out yet. So as NCCICS is pushing out these alerts in real time, I cannot share those until I get to a full-blown ISAC.

But this whole concept of sharing and collaboration is just huge, and getting as near-real-time as we can, because the goal is we don't want to be reactive. We want to get proactive, so we want to know everything we can coming from all the services that provide this type of information, so that we can then take a proactive stance to protect our systems.

Mr. FITZPATRICK. Special Agent Quinn from the FBI indicated in his testimony that some institutions would be reluctant from reporting. Now, Mr. Peters, you talked about, in your industry, you are required to report.

Mr. PETERS. Yes.

Mr. FITZPATRICK. The FBI—he indicated some might be reluctant to support, I suspect because competitors would take advantage of that lapse in security. Is that your understanding?

Mr. PETERS. I don't know that I can speak to the reluctance. I mean, one of the things, from working with the Secret Service, is these Electronic Crimes Task Force, and getting that information out to the retailers so that they establish a relationship with that organization, so that, when they do get the call, it is not necessarily, you know, hello, this is the Secret Service calling you. It is, hello, this is Ari calling you, yeah, what is up? We have that ability, and that relationship, so that we are comfortable now working with law enforcement and moving forward.

Again, from the breach notification perspective, it is the problem of all the different laws in the States that we have, that we are trying to now figure out, what do I have to do?

Mr. FITZPATRICK. Thank you.

Mr. MEEHAN. I thank Mr. Fitzpatrick. Let me just ask a follow-up question. Mr. Rhoades, you—your testimony speaks to an issue which, as I alluded to in my first line of questioning with the earlier panel, but it is still—again, it is very, very disconcerting that the median time——

Mr. RHOADES. Um-hum.

Mr. MEEHAN [continuing]. That—days before someone appreciates businesses or otherwise that there is, you know, there is activity within—inside their networks is 229 days, median, before it is recognized. In addition, we are seeing, particularly from the Eastern European, that, once in the system, they are using that window to create software that mimics the actual operation of the entity——

Mr. RHOADES. Um-hum.

Mr. MEEHAN [continuing]. Which makes it even more difficult. So are we walking into a period here where detection is going to become increasingly more difficult, and longer, and therefore a greater opportunity for compromise?

Mr. RHOADES. I don't know if detection will become longer. The report that I cited in my written testimony, the 229 days, while staggering and very long, was actually an improvement over what that security provider had found in the previous year by about 2 weeks. The adversaries are becoming more sophisticated, though, so it may be more difficult to notice them. This is especially true for—you mentioned earlier a non-profit. There has been some conversation around small businesses. One of the things—the previous panel was enlightening. I thought one of the things that was missing was the human power that is required to do these things.

So, technology is nice. Technology really, in this space, only enables policies and processes for an individual, business, or entity to protect itself. Cybersecurity, at its core, eventually comes down to people. So, to have trained people to understand when they receive information from others, how they can actually incorporate that and protect their networks, to have people that are trained to use the technologies that they have so that they can detect anomalies in their networks, I think that is the fundamental challenge, especially with small businesses and non-profits. That is the biggest challenge for these actors getting more sophisticated.

I think the technologies will advance to be able to pick up some of these network anomalies, but do you have an individual on the other side watching that that can sort of understand what to do with that information?

Mr. MEEHAN. Let me take it from the other side, which is the information that is collected. I mean, we are now dealing collectively in Washington with an issue regarding personal information, the recognition that the Government, in certain capacities, may be tracking if you made a phone call.

Mr. RHOADES. Um-hum.

Mr. MEEHAN. Yet what strikes me is, while that is an important privacy question that we have to deal with, the wealth of information that is being collected about our activities out there in the cyber world, consumer world, or wherever, is overwhelming——

Mr. RHOADES. Um-hum.

Mr. MEEHAN [continuing]. So much so that people are looking at tendencies, they are looking at the ability to know a great deal more about us than ever before. So where is the boundary with respect to what is appropriate to collect about individuals without a corresponding obligation——

Mr. RHOADES. Right.

Mr. MEEHAN [continuing]. For security? Looking at the University of Maryland situation, where, you know, they kept legacy information for some 300,000 people, where is there some cyber hygiene going where people are determining that, you know, a certain amount of information is all that is needed, and we are going to excise all the unnecessary information? Seems we are going in opposite directions.

Mr. RHOADES. Yeah, I think certainly the individual is losing control over our private information going forward. I can remember the first time I was at a particular retailer, and I purchased a bottle of wine, and they scanned my driver's license. That was without asking. That was just part of their policy. I wasn't given the opportunity to necessarily agree or disagree with it, or to question what information was being collected. I still, to this day, am not quite sure what they store for how long, and how it is used. That is a—that is not to pick on a particular retailer. I think that is now a common case, that there are entities, some legitimate, some illegitimate, that are taking this information and using it to monetize.

So I think this is—there is a new emphasis, particularly over the course of the past 12 months, in the American public dialogue on privacy and civil liberties. I think, as these technologies advance, we need a broader National conversation about what we feel is appropriate, and we feel is maybe too much, and to find a way for individuals to somehow gain a little bit, or feel they have gained a little bit more control over their private information.

Mr. MEEHAN. Who controls that? Who becomes the arbiter of that, and how is that enforced?

Mr. RHOADES. Well, the overall arbiter, ideally, would be the American people. Having this conversation, particularly through you all, our representatives, and deciding what is appropriate, and what is not. That often does not—is not the way things work, I understand that, but I think that this is where we, as average citizens, particularly look to you to represent our best interests.

Mr. MEEHAN. Well, I thank you. Do any of my colleagues have any follow-up questions? Chairman recognizes Ms. Clarke.

Ms. CLARKE. Thank you, Mr. Chairman, and I want to agree with you on the need to have this conversation. I wonder how much of this debate is generational——

Mr. RHOADES. Um-hum.

Ms. CLARKE [continuing]. Simply because younger people live their lives through this medium——

Mr. RHOADES. Um-hum.

Ms. CLARKE [continuing]. In a way that perhaps my parents, and even me, to a certain degree, don't. You know, I am a hybrid. My mom is all-in now, she is texting. But, you know, there is a conversation that needs to be had, because things that we believe are private, young people don't necessarily believe the same thing. So when you transfer that into the final arbiter, which in—oftentimes are the courts now, the application of current day law to what they are actually doing, there is a disconnect. You know, because—there is almost a voluntary surrender of privacy through this medium in certain parts of the internet, social networking, for instance, and so that conversation needs to happen, because I am just concerned that we establish a standard so that people can then gauge themselves accordingly. I think at a certain point it is going to become almost moot, because everyone's information is going to be out there, so it is going to cancel out.

But, having said that, data breaches involve personally identifiable information, as the Chairman has stated, and under many circumstances, and for many reasons, they can be inadvertent, such as from the loss of an electronic device, or deliberate, such as from a theft of a device, or a cyber-based attack by a malicious individual or group for a nation, a terrorist, or the adversary. Incidents have been reported at a wide range of public-private sector institutions, including Federal, State, local government agencies, educational institutions, hospitals, other medical facilities, financial institutions, retailers, et cetera.

The loss or unauthorized disclosure or alteration of the information residing in private and public systems, which include this PII, can lead to serious consequences and substantial harm to individuals in the Nation. It is critical that not only Federal agencies, but privately-owned companies also protect their systems, and the information on them, and to respond to data breaches and cyber incidents when they occur. The President asked, in his cybersecurity Executive Order, 136–36, that there be a separate section on privacy, civil liberty protections, and PII. It contains a new subsection, entitled, "Methodology To Protect Privacy and Civil Liberties", and is Appendix B of the primary framework.

Could you give us an update——

Mr. RHOADES. Um-hum.

Ms. CLARKE. You know, I threw out sort-of my thinking, and, you know, I am left-handed. But, you know, what do you think the update on the discussion is, and the collaboration among public and private entities regarding privacy and civil liberty concerns?

Mr. RHOADES. Sure. So, as you mentioned, in the Executive Order the President asked, through the programs that are implemented under that Order, for the senior privacy and civil liberties officers at each of the agencies involved to look at those programs and do a risk-based assessment, in terms of privacy and civil liberties, and to offer some strategies going forward to mitigate some of those risks.

I believe earlier this week, or it may have been last week, the Department of Homeland Security released its first assessment of that, which, to me, it—I think that is an important point for two reasons. No. 1, it gives, for those of you who do oversight over the administration, the opportunity to sort of baseline these things, look at some of their recommendations that are in-house, and then follow those as we go forward to ensure they have been implemented.

But I also think that is an important document strictly from an emphasis on privacy and civil liberties. The specific recommendations didn't necessarily stand out to me as game changers, but in terms of getting overall cybersecurity right, this is a real challenge, in that it requires trust at every level.

I think, through both panels of this hearing, we have heard there are multiple levers of—level of users, from nation-states, to big corporations, to small corporations, to non-profits, to individual end-users. I agree with the Chairman when he said that this is a shared responsibility, so all of these levels must work together. Frankly, here we have seen less trust from the average American citizen to the Federal Government. So I think it is important domestically to start to rebuild some of that trust, particularly in light of the National conversation over the last year.

I also think it is really important internationally, because, as I said, we are the first generation to sort of try to develop the doctrines and the concepts around these new technologies. The fact is the rest of the world is watching us as we struggle to come up with those ideas. How we do things here in the United States is going to greatly affect the next Green Movement in Iran, the next Tahrir Square, so we need to be very cognizant of those as well if we do still want to stand for some of those fundamental American rights of individual opportunity, of individual freedom, of free speech.

So I think, for those reasons, that emphasis in the E.O., and then the most recent report is important. But then I would also encourage you all to look at some of the recommendations, and to ensure that the Executive follows up on their own assessments.

Ms. CLARKE. Thank you, Mr. Chairman. I yield back.

Mr. MEEHAN. Well, I want to express my deep appreciation to each of you, not just for your preparation for your testimony today, and the work, and—you have put into those thoughtful comments, but for your on-going work in this area in each of your respective venues. It is a debate—not a debate, it is a dialogue that we are going to have to be continuing well into the future. I want to express my appreciation to our colleagues, and particularly my—the Ranking Member for taking the time to travel here from New York.

I want to close by thanking our hosts here at Drexel, and for the tremendous work that they are doing in being on the vanguard in both—not just education, but research and development in this important area of cybersecurity. I am grateful for their efforts.

So, on behalf of the committee, the subcommittee stands adjourned.

[Whereupon, at 12:49 p.m., the subcommittee was adjourned.]

○